The Momentous Leap

Thriveable Transformation in the 21st Century:

Healing Ourselves, Healing our Planet

Dr Robin Lincoln Wood

© **Dr Robin Lincoln Wood**

2018

Illustrations for the Six Pathways by Kirstie Eloise Wood
Diagrams and models by the author

Other Books by Dr Robin Wood

Making Good Happen – Pathways to a Thriving Future - 2017

Synergise! 21st Century Leadership – 2017

A Leaders Guide to ThriveAbility – 2015

*The Trouble with Paradise: A Humorous Enquiry Into the Puzzling
Human Condition in the 21st Century - 2014*

LifeShift 2020 – 2009

The Great Shift: Catalyzing the Second Renaissance - 2009

*Managing Complexity:
How Businesses can Adapt and Prosper in the Connected Economy
– 2000*

**Visit the author's amazon page for more details:
www.amazon.com/author/woodrobin**

The Momentous Leap – An Overview

The Momentous Leap, the 7th book by award winning author Dr Robin Lincoln Wood, explores the most exciting transition humanity has ever experienced. Right now, across our planet, people are developing worldcentric, systemic perspectives and capabilities that will not only resolve most of the challenges we currently face – they will also transform our species and what it means to be human.

Imagine a world powered by renewable energy, where all human beings thrive in resilient habitats; where businesses operate in a circular economy that regenerates natural capital, without a particle of waste, led by enlightened leaders whose goal is to maximize the thriving of all stakeholders; where each individual is empowered to pursue their passion and make a living in service to others; where governance systems are transparent, effective and wise in the ways in which they deliver their services to their communities and populations; and where intercultural appreciation and insight enriches the exchanges between the diverse worldviews and cultures embraced by humankind.

Does that sound like an impossible dream? Every single one of these "pockets of the future" is currently observable in the present, right here and right now, somewhere in the world. This exceptional book is a guide for those who wish to understand and take part in this global transformation, showing us how to connect and align with the pockets of the future in the present that will become mainstream reality for most of us by 2030. You will also discover the roots of the rapidly growing regenerative, distributive economy, along with the emerging social and political systems that can ensure a thriving future for us all, and a flourishing biosphere for all life on earth.

You will learn how to transcend and master the apparent chaos and complexity inherent in our globalized, post-modern world, so that you can not only adapt to the massive shifts underway, but also help shape them. Despite the doom and gloom of many today, there are 700 million plus people leading the way toward a thriveable future- what Peter Drucker called: "Getting into our strategic psychological helicopter and transcending the problem", enabling challenges to be viewed from multiple perspectives and producing breakthroughs at emergent, unprecedented levels of thinking.

You will discover how enlightened mainstream leaders (many still "undercover"), are shifting their policies, businesses and investments toward renewable energy, resilient cities, circular economies and conscious leadership; and how those making the leap from the cultural creative world also number in the many millions, especially the activists, organisers and civil society leaders. You will also learn of the artistic, cultural, design and social leaders inspiring a tsunami of talent doing well by doing good, dedicated to making a better world and a positive difference, along with the younger generations now surfing this big wave, embracing a broad diversity of visionary actors of all ages that are reshaping whole social, economic, cultural and educational systems in more holistic, joined up ways.

We are operating in a turbulent field of social transformation. The ride is guaranteed to be full of shocks and surprises, as well as amazing new opportunities. You can be a part of a thriving future that regenerates our biosphere and our global civilisation to be a more peaceful, sustainable and enjoyable place to live. The rewards of healing yourself, and healing our planet at the same time, are immense. No matter where you are on your own journey, applying the thinking and frameworks in this book to improve your own practices and skills will help you become more focused and powerful in your efforts. Your fellow travelers are already out there, waiting for you to connect up with them, and make the momentous leap together.

Robin Lincoln Wood

Perpignan

August 2018

TABLE OF CONTENTS

The Momentous Leap

The first two decades of the 21st century have been a bumpy ride for most of us. Yet we seem to be on the cusp of a profound transformation in what it means to be human. History buffs know that what it means to be human has changed several times in our brief sojourn on earth as homo sapiens- and that each new wave of being more human has always brought with it both blessings and curses. What blessings and curses will the new ways of being human in the 21st century bring?

Five thousand years ago there were about five million of us, scraping a living off the land, ruled by Kings, Emperors, priests and landlords. The natural world was flourishing, offering us an abundance of wilderness and domesticated animals. Most of us lived on farms and in small villages, and while being blessed with a close connection with nature, we also suffered from regular famines and invasions by barbarian hordes, as well as a vulnerability to diseases that brought often short and brutal lives.

Five hundred years ago, there were nearly five hundred million of us, with one in three of us living in a town or a large city. The natural world was still flourishing, though living conditions in towns and cities were very basic for almost all of us. Running water, hot baths, plumbing, indoor toilets and sewers were still waiting to be installed in most urban centres of the world, and life was still quite short, nasty and often brutish, as anyone who has ever read a play by the leading playwright at that time, William Shakespeare, can attest.

In the 21st century, there are now more than 7.5 billion of us humans, along with several hundred billion domesticated animals. By 2050 seven out of ten of us will be living in one of the 5 000 cities that will then dominate our planet, and there may be another two or so billion people added to our number at that time. And if we continue business-as usual, we may end up using three planets worth of resources to stay alive in increasingly difficult, challenging conditions as rising sea levels, droughts, heat waves, mega-storms, mass extinctions and mass migrations take their toll on us.

Most of us are now familiar with the disaster scenarios that proliferate in our media and conversations in the developed world, while those living in the developing world are increasingly experiencing those disasters in their daily lives. On the one hand we are heading for extinction, or a world where being human will be like living in a combination of the Matrix, Bladerunner, Elysium and Mad Max movies. On the other hand, we may be able to scale the transformation we are seeing in a few hundred million people and in hundreds of thousands of places and projects, so that we create a thriving future for life on earth and ourselves.

This scenario of a thriving future is a real possibility, if we can grasp what the momentous leap is and how we can become an active part of it. The promise is captivating, the alternative disastrous. So, what do you need to be able to know and do, to make this thriving future a reality for yourself and others?

PART 1. THE MOMENTOUS LEAP – WHAT, WHY, WHERE

1. Momentous Leaps Are Us

We humans are the product of several momentous leaps in evolution. Many of our fellow living creatures on earth have barely evolved for hundreds of millions of years. For example, in 1938 a natural history curator in South Africa called Marjorie Courtenay-Latimer realized that a fish she was examining should not have existed. The fish belonged to a group that was thought to have gone extinct 65 million years ago, during the same cataclysm that wiped out the dinosaurs. It was a coelacanth.

Coelacanths have roots that stretch back 390 million years. They are large, bottom-dwelling fish that can grow up to 2m long. Their fleshy, limb-like fins and dappled scales look as if they've been flecked with blobs of white paint. They are the only survivors of the lobe-finned fishes, a group that once dominated the oceans. In 2013 scientists sequenced the genome of the African coelacanth. They found that it is the closest living relative of the first land animals that began to appear 400 million years ago.

Equally cockroaches, some sharks, cycads, horseshoe crabs and the tadpole shrimp have survived largely unchanged for some three hundred million years. Why is that some creatures can survive, even flourish for such vast lengths of time? In some cases their environments did not change very much- in others they were simply very fast adaptors.

We humans are some of the fastest evolving creatures on the planet. Around 40,000 years ago, the human population exploded, and evolution sped up. In 2007, John Hawks of the

University of Wisconsin, Madison and his colleagues studied the DNA from 270 individuals and found that human evolution "has recently accelerated by 100-fold".

Similarly, a 2014 study estimated that the most recent common ancestor of all living humans lived around 239,000 years ago. That is much more recent than some estimates, and again suggests that humans have been evolving rapidly. Even within the last 10,000 years, humans have changed. The existence of blue eyes, and the ability of some adults to drink animal milk that contains lactose, are two examples of recent biological innovations.

But what has helped humans evolve faster than any other species ever, is our culture and our technology. We have domesticated some 220 animals, birds and fish for a variety of purposes, for example, by passing on the ability from generation to generation to selectively breed and interbreed different species to give us the features we find most useful or pleasant. Through urbanization and climate change we are also now dramatically altering the habitats of hundreds of thousands of species, some of which are adapting, and others which are sadly going extinct in the sixth mass extinction.

While humans continue to evolve bio-physically, we are evolving even faster culturally and technologically. Much as a spider weaves a web to help it catch food, so we have woven a worldwide web of technology and cultural innovations that makes life more secure, comfortable and pleasant for us. Yet our very success as the top predator on earth is also one of the reasons we are now experiencing the challenges of climate change and causing the sixth mass extinction. We may have made several leaps to get where we are today, but the most momentous of all leaps is now required for us to enable us to look forward to a thriving future. What might that leap look like, and will we make it?

2. A Game of Leapfrog

Leapfrog is originally a game in which players take turns to vault with parted legs over others who are bending down. The concept of leapfrogging is used in many different domains of economics and business and was originally developed in the field of industrial organization and economic growth. Leap Frog strategy is defined as way to surpass or overthrow superior competition by engaging in a determined, brilliant leap that results in extraordinary growth and success.

One of the most hopeful aspects of our current situation is that human, cultural and socio-technical developments can literally "jump" from one state to another, given the right conditions. Some simple organisms such as slime moulds become a single colony when facing life-threatening conditions, for example. All social creatures can amplify their collective intelligence by forming real-time synchronous systems. These natural gatherings include flocks, schools, shoals, blooms, colonies, herds, and swarms.

Such highly coordinated behaviours are the product of millions of years of evolution that conferred survival benefits on a great many species. In this way, nature demonstrates that social creatures, by functioning together in closed-loop systems, can outperform the vast majority of individual members when solving problems and making decisions, thereby boosting overall survival of their population.

In human beings we can see leapfrog in action in many different contexts. For example, in the field of technology, mobile telephone networks enable developing countries to leapfrog fixed telephone and data lines. Solar, wind and biofuel renewable energy technologies ensure that we can bypass coal, gas and oil for our energy needs.

Social technologies, in particular, can be a powerful agent of leapfrog through collective intelligence. In truly collaborative forms of social media, content is not just shared by groups but created by groups working together as an emergent intelligence. This may provide us with a more human-friendlier alternative to traditional Artificial Intelligence, for swarming kinds of social interactions can build new intelligences while keeping humans in the loop.

All technologies are ultimately the product of our individual and social imaginations and creativity. As human consciousness matures and develops into more complex and adaptive forms, so we create more evolutionary pathways that may make it possible for us to leapfrog over current ways of doing things that are literally, costing the earth. We may in turn find new ways of living and working together more harmoniously and effectively than ever before.

What is often called "sustainable innovation" has taken off in the past few decades in developing countries, building on "bottom-of-the pyramid", lean business models that are able to deliver healthcare and surgery at one-tenth the cost in the developed world; or mobile phone services that cost less than

$10 a month in India; or micro-cars that cost less than a month's salary of an average western worker.

Such lean innovations offer great hope for our future, as they help bring down the use of our precious natural and human resources to more sustainable, even thriveable levels. Together with all the other incredible breakthroughs scaling up right now in many millions of projects and businesses, traditional Artificial Intelligence and synergistic Collective Intelligence platforms offer powerful ways to make our momentous leap a reality.

3. The Leap has Already Begun

The leap in the world of socio-technical systems has been the most obvious and dramatic we have observed in the past century, as has the cost of that leap in terms of natural and human capitals. Yet, hidden not far below the surface of our materialistic, consumer-driven global economic system, we can find another leap that is much less obvious: a transformation in the values and consciousness of a large proportion of the human race.

This transformation is not only redefining what we mean by the "good life"- it is also shifting our lifestyles to more sustainable and healthier ways of being, with an emphasis on wellbeing and thriving, rather than simply consuming and disposing endlessly. Such shifts in both conventional and post-conventional ways of living are adaptations to external drivers- for example, rising prices driving those with more traditional values to conserve and switch to lower-impact products and services; and internal drivers- for example, cultural creatives seeking inner peace through voluntary simplicity.

There are several hundred million cultural creatives across the globe- by 2020 cultural creatives could be over half of the American population, with a few hundred million more spread throughout Europe and the world's major cities. Yet, interestingly enough, they often feel they are alone, as traditionalists and modernists surround them. While traditionalists stage their last stand in right-wing politics, they are literally dying out as most are now over sixty in the developed world.

Modernists, meanwhile, are trending toward cultural creative activities, as self-actualization becomes a priority for them. For example, in the 1970s yoga and meditation were considered "alternative", but now form a vital part of progressive Modernist practices. Culture nurtures our souls and binds our communities together, while creativity helps reveal new answers to our challenges and anxieties. Industries that build on creativity and culture are also a source of great economic value and societal well-being.

In Europe for example, culture and creativity lie at the heart of policy making. Sound policies are applied to promote cultural diversity, protect cultural heritage and support the contribution of cultural and creative industries to boosting job creation and growth. The Cultural and Creative Cities Monitor is at the heart of this effort. It is designed to help cities identify their strengths and opportunities, benchmark their performance and push for policies to close gaps. Its vast pool of comparable data leads to new insights into the impact of culture and creativity on cities' well-being and provide a toolbox for engaged citizens to improve their lot.

Over the past century we've also see the emergence of more complex levels of human development from the growing pool of cultural creatives- a kind of complex, integrative, realistic intelligence and way of being that transcends any situation while including its essential ingredients in novel ways. According to decades of research by psychologist Professor Clare Graves, this way of thinking and being started showing up strongly in his multi-decadal data in the 1960's. One of its most notable features is the absence of fear, together with the ability to see the world from multiple perspectives and value systems.

The list of the pioneers of this complex, integrative, evolutionary realistic way of thinking and being include Albert Einstein, Buckminster Fuller, Jan Smuts, Pierre Teilhard de Chardin, Sri Auribindo, Henri Bergson, Alfred North Whitehead, Jean Gebser, Goethe, Brian Swimme, Barbara Marx Hubbard, Peter Russell, Ken Wilber and Don Beck, amongst many other distinguished scientists, philosophers, mystics and futurists.

4. Why This Leap Matters

During the 1960's and 1970's there was a growing awareness amongst political, cultural, business and scientific leaders around the globe that the spread of nuclear weapons and our excessive exploitation of the earth's precious resources might spell the end of humanity as we know it. As Albert Einstein had put it a few decades earlier:

"The world we have made, as a result of the level of thinking we have done thus far, creates problems we cannot solve at the same level of thinking at which we created them."

In 1974, the American psychologist Clare Graves published a paper entitled 'Human Nature Prepares for a Momentous Leap' in which he argued that human society is facing a period of fundamental change, "the most difficult, but at the same time the most exciting transition the human race has faced to date." Graves believed that humanity was at the beginning of "not merely a transition to a new level of existence, but the start of a new movement in the symphony of human history".

According to Graves' predictions, humanity had to collectively make a conscious choice between three distinct possibilities for the future of human society:

- A massive regression back to Stone Age beginnings if we fail to stabilize our world's weapons and endangered resources.
- A version of George Orwell's 1984, embodied in forms of tyrannical, manipulative governments with glossed over communitarian overtones.
- The emergence of a Second-Tier approach to business and society which would be fundamentally different from the one we know today, equipped to act locally and plan globally while acting globally and planning locally at the same time.

After more than a quarter century of research into how humans live, act, engage in decision- making processes, and change as participants of complex systems, Graves provided a dynamic map of the developmental stages of human consciousness, value systems and worldviews. He described a number of behavioural systems, based on the biological, psychological and social way of relating to the wider world—the whole—that these "biopsychosocial systems" result in.

Graves described this leap as follows in this article for the Futurist magazine in 1974:

"As man moves from the sixth or personalistic level, the level of being with self and other men, the seventh level, the cognitive level of existence, a chasm of unbelievable depth of meaning is crossed. The gap between the sixth level and the seventh level is the gap between getting and giving, taking and contributing, destroying and constructing. It is the gap between deficiency or deficit motivation and growth or abundance motivation. It is the gap between similarity to animals and dissimilarity to animals, because only man is possessed of a future orientation."

This momentous leap matters because the survival of humankind and much of the biosphere depends on it. World leaders agree that we need to make fundamental shifts in every aspect of our existence in the next decade or so, which requires a fundamental shift in the consciousness of our leaders, ourselves and the cultures we currently operate from and in.

5. Where the Leap is At

The momentous leap takes many forms and can be observed shape-shifting as it emerges and evolves in various parts of the world. The scientists, mystics and philosophers appear to have begun articulating more complex, integrative, evolutionary and realistic ways of thinking and being more than a century ago, and this has indeed strongly shaped the emergence of modernism and post-modernism and our globalized modern world as we know it.

By the turn of the 21st century, what pre-eminent management guru Peter Drucker called: "Getting into our strategic psychological helicopter and transcending the problem" became more in evidence in executive and political corridors of power. This enabled challenges to be viewed from multiple perspectives, producing solutions at emergent levels of thinking that had never been tried before.

There are slightly over one million people who run the global political economy. These are among the 1.5 million readers of the Economist magazine, and also the millions of leaders who actively own and manage most of the world's financial, infrastructure and manufactured capital. Some of these leaders are part of the leap, remaining largely "undercover" as they shift their policies, businesses and investments toward renewable energy, resilient cities, circular economies and conscious leadership - although more are now coming out into the open as this way of doing things becomes more mainstream. These are the *enlightened mainstream leaders*.

Those making the leap from the cultural creative world also number in the many millions, especially the activists, organisers and civil society leaders. Together with artistic, cultural, design and social leaders, we see a tsunami of talent bent on doing well by doing good, dedicated to making a better world and a positive difference. The *Millennials* are the latest ripple on this big wave of visionary actors of all ages reshaping social, economic, cultural and educational systems in more holistic, joined up ways.

The historical roots of the leap straddle West and East, North and South. In particular, the synthesis in the past century between eastern mystical and western rational traditions has enriched both sides, and given rise to much that is now taken for granted in helping accelerate the momentous leap, whether it be depth psychology, meditation, mindfulness, various forms of yoga, together with other practices that have become an essential part of what is now often called "integral" or "second-tier" ways of thinking, being & doing.

While several hundred million *cultural creatives* and the tens of millions of *enlightened mainstream leaders* in science, business, politics and civil society are making the leap now and in the next few decades, we are seeing a great shift in what is considered to be acceptable and desirable in our collective evolution, and a deepening of our ability to make good happen along clearly defined pathways to a thriving future. Slowly, but surely, we are able to take more seriously our emerging ability to transform what is not working and to renew and cherish what is, so that we can manage the massive challenges and opportunities posed by this new movement in the symphony of human history.

PART 2: LEAPING THROUGH THE CHAORDIC ZONE

6. We Live in Confusing, Unsettling Times

Most people are struggling to make sense of the rapid unfolding of events and shifts that have taken place in the first few decades of the 21st century. A few billion employed people, investors, politicians and business owners are experiencing unprecedented comfort, security and convenience. Meanwhile, a few billion of us are struggling to make ends meet and survive, and another few billion are suffering in various ways from hunger, poverty, lack of water and few prospects of things getting any better.

A century ago, almost the entire planet was ruled by colonial Empires, and their Emperors, Kings and Queens. There were a few exceptions, ruled by elected Presidents, including America. People "knew their place", and it was more or less accepted that the rich would get richer and the poor would have children. Then, in less than a century, all that changed. 76 countries are now full or slightly flawed democracies (North and Latin America plus Western Europe), while 40 are hybrid regimes (in Asia, Central/Eastern Europe and Sub-Saharan Africa) and 51 are authoritarian regimes (most in the Middle East and Northern Africa).

The 20th century saw almost half the world shift from autocratic to democratic systems of governance, while also seeing average incomes per person rise five times in developed countries and 2.5 times in developing countries. It seemed that the magic combination of a mixed economy and democracy plus rising levels of education were delivering prosperity for all. Until the dotcom bubble burst in 2000, it seemed that progress was inevitable everywhere.

During the first two decades of the 21st century, however, things started going backwards. In this time there has been a failure of democracy in 25 countries, together with subtle degradations in democratic rights in a number of western democracies. At the same time, The Gini coefficient, a standard measure of income inequality[i], increased by almost 10% between 1980 to 2010.

While the incomes of the world's poorest have risen substantially in countries like China and India in the past fifty years, the middle classes have seen their incomes and wealth decline sharply in the last few decades in developed economies, causing the rise of populism and general dissatisfaction with the "system", as the wealth of the richest ten percent has grown by leaps and bounds.

The clashes between the rising tide of liberal/socialist *cultural creative* values, neo-liberal/ *conservative modernist* values and the backlash of *traditional* values segments of populations everywhere, combined with rising inequality and uncertainty, has led to a potentially explosive situation where everyone is unhappy with the direction things are going in, with only the top 10% laughing uneasily all the way to the bank. But even the levels of happiness in this segment are not rising, as a great deal of pressure is now on the richest 10% to help improve the overall situation and also pay their fair share of taxes.

On top of all this, we find the lowest levels of trust in politics, business and the establishment in general, ever, and rising threats from climate change and over-consumption of the earth's precious resources driving unprecedented suffering due to heat waves, droughts, wildfires, floods, extreme storms, rising sea levels and the exhaustion of our food supplies, soil and oceans looming. No wonder life seems to be more confusing and harder than ever for so many of us. Where is this all going, and what can we possibly do to make things better, we ask ourselves? Let's begin by developing a more powerful model that can helps us understand the major shifts that are driving the momentous leap right now around the planet.

7. Leaps Happen between Layers in Stratified Systems

The history of humankind comprises a series of momentous leaps between successive layers of increasingly complex ways of being. Right now we are at one of the major turning points for our species. The decisions we make going forward, especially in the next decade, will shape the future of homo sapiens and life on earth for many centuries, if not millennia, to come.

Geology, evolution, cultures and progress all have one thing in common: they are laid down one layer at a time, so that it is possible to see the different layers from the oldest to the newest, the oldest at the bottom and the newest at the top, if we dig deep enough. These layers, or "strata", give rise to the name we give these systems: "Stratified systems".

Each time a new layer is added to a stratified system, new materials and a large amount of energy are mixed into a solution that eventually solidifies under pressure to become the next layer in the system. Take a look at what we call the geological record, or the fossil record to see these different layers, graphically arranged before your eyes. Gravity compresses them together over time.

In human stratified systems we can most easily see the layers of civilisation through ancient archaeological sites, whether ancient Greek temples in the Mediterranean, or the Roman walls emerging in parts of the City of London. Within several vertical metres one can see thousands of years of history piled on top of each other, layer by layer. Each layer represents a hundred or so years of human events, from the first marble stones laid for the first temple, to the ruins left by fires and conquests, to the next layer of wooden houses in Shakespeare's time, until we find the red bricks of Victorian days and then the concrete and steel of modern times.

Stratified systems that are invisible to the naked eye are, however, much harder for the layperson to see or understand, much as the workings of the human body were a mystery until the practice of anatomy and dissection revealed the many systems comprising the living human organism. When we attempt to understand the needs, values, priorities and intentions of living systems and how they interact and co-evolve with the other stratified systems that constitute their life conditions, we must resort to maps and models with sufficient dimensionality to represent such interactions and their outcomes.

We must not only scale up the technological and scientific solutions needed to avert a global catastrophe- we must go deeper to redesign and shift our psychological, organisational and social habits as part of the next momentous leap. The significant breakthroughs in biology, psychology, neurology, cognitive science and sociology in the past century, enable us to better map and model the interactions between living and stratified systems of all kinds. This has given us deep insights into the evolution of life, civilisation and our species, together with some predictive powers that have helped us design better life conditions and interactions that are conducive to thriving rather than struggling and suffering.

Our beautiful blue pearl of spaceship earth is host to 7.6 billion earthlings, in the midst of at least eight major transitions through four eras. The "Momentous Leap" describes the leap into Era 4 - the post-global, post-modern leap to a distributed network of globally interconnected but autonomous projects and programs that not only knit together the best of diverse eras and cultures, but at the same time ensure this is done so as to enhance the ability of each autonomous unit to thrive in its own unique way. In other words: "Think global, act local and synergise the interactions of diverse eras and cultures to produce beneficial, thriveable outcomes locally and globally".

8. The Momentous Leap Transcends & Includes 3 Eras

The momentous leap taking place right now across our globe is being driven by the rising tide of *cultural creative* values and liberal/socialist tendencies in the younger generations, comprising somewhere in the order of a billion people. Those in the mainstream with *progressive modernist* values are also shifting toward complex, integrative, realistic ways of thinking and doing, while there is a predictable backlash of *traditional* values segments of populations everywhere who feel left behind and ignored by both the cultural creatives and the progressive modernists.

The key feature of the momentous leap we are now in is the joined-up nature of complex, integrative, realistic ways of thinking and doing. This co-creative, networked way of generating distributed power amongst globally interconnected but autonomous projects and programs knits together the best of diverse eras and cultures to create beneficial outcomes. What is often called an "integral approach" integrates the best of human capabilities that we have developed over the past 20 000 years of our evolution. We humans possess tremendous adaptive capacities, grounded in our having already transitioned through three major evolutionary eras:

Era 1 - Tribal/Traditional - We must build on our ability to forge strong bonds to ensure our local survival and thriving.

These *ethnocentric* bonds and expressive talents are native to all of us, enabling us to take care of each other and the places we care for and hold sacred, while also exploring and connecting with nature and each other at a local level.

Era 2 - Modern/City-Nation States - We can build on our ability to manage cities, regions and nation states in more thriveable ways, respecting the rule of law and building intelligent infrastructures and systems fit for the future, based on enlightened entrepreneurship, conscious business sense and innovation. These *civic-centric* and *enterprise-centric* talents are increasingly evident around the world, from the developed nations to what were previously termed "developing countries".

Era 3 – Post-Modern/Global – Finally, we can build on our ability to evolve our global systems embodied in our global treaties, international institutions, corporations, markets and flows of people, goods, information and goodwill, so that our global systems also become a driver of a thriveable future for us all. These *world-centric* talents are now evident in nearly one billion global citizens, who are sufficiently educated and travelled that they can appreciate the glorious diversity of our species and other species.

As we enter **Era 4**, we now have the capacity to rapidly accelerate the evolution of our species, based on thriveable cultures, mindsets, principles and metrics. The forces and trends shaping our world and us are creating crises that demand a momentous leap from our previously lose-lose/win-lose "us versus them" mentality, to a co-creative, collaborative win/win/win approach.

This "triple win" is fundamental to aligning the interests and mindsets of all people on the planet, whatever kind of transition they are in and whatever their era: a win for each of us as individuals and for our communities, a win for the cities/towns/nations we live in, and a win for the planet as a whole. That is the whole point of the synergistic innovation driving integral approaches: co-creating triple wins that generate thriveable futures and ensure a viable biosphere and life conditions for us all by 2050. On the way to this co-creative triple-win Era 4, however, we must navigate the chaordic zone.

9. Transitioning the Chaordic Zone

As described earlier, leaps occur between layers in civilisations, cultures and species, and a few billion of us are currently struggling with a degree of confusion about where things are actually heading. This is "situation normal" in any leap. Why?

Each time a new layer is added to a stratified system, *new materials* and a *large amount of energy* are mixed into a solution that eventually solidifies under pressure to become the next layer in the system. In a human stratified system, the new materials include novel perspectives, technologies, resources and materials, together with the mixing of diverse races, cultures, languages and ideas.

The mixing of these new materials takes place in a variety of containers or "crucibles", where what is known in evolutionary theory as "peripheral isolates" form new combinations that constitute "pockets of the future in the present". In biology and cultures, peripheral isolates are found isolated on the periphery of larger populations. They are potentially subject to different selective pressures and, because of their location, are most likely to become cut off from the larger population due to the formation of geographical or other barriers or, instead, due to a shrinking of the range of the larger, parental population.

Historically, some of these peripheral isolate populations survive, spread and ultimately become a new mainstream over several generations. In our hyper-mediated world, we also know much more about these "pockets of the future in the present", due to global communications networks and news media, so that those in mainstream populations who are more open and attracted to these new ways of living and being can adopt new ideas, practices and technologies themselves, without even meeting a member of the peripheral isolate group.

The extensive variety of interactions between mainstream populations and peripheral isolates in the 21st century consumes and also generates enormous amounts of biophysical and human energy. The "edge of chaos" conditions that occur in the most intense of these interactions are often cognitively and emotionally overwhelming, especially for those who are emotionally and psychologically vulnerable and less resistant to stronger minds and dogmas.

These less resistant groups are often swept up in movements, cults, conspiracy theories and religions that can be fanatical or extreme in one or more ways, so that they are effectively "brainwashed" and immune to reason or facts contradicting their new belief system. They often seek safety in numbers. The more cognitively and emotionally robust will seek to navigate their way through the chaordic zone through accelerated learning and collective intelligence solutions, though this makes the ride no less bumpy and the journey no less turbulent or risky.

As the selection pressures of changed life conditions begin to operate on these new varieties of ways of being human, some make it through to the next generations because they have evolved effective adaptations, while others wither gradually or perish suddenly in various extinction events. This is not only happening to humans right now, but also to all the other species on our planet as they strive to adapt to rapid climate change. The chaordic zone is real for tens of millions of species, including us.

For human beings, the chaordic zone is a place where we can expend a great deal of energy and resources while remaining trapped in unproductive places and unpleasant situations, which is why a deeper understanding of its dynamics are so key to our ability to survive and thrive.

10. The Dynamics of the Chaordic Zone

Dee Hock, the founder of VISA, coined the term "chaordic". Hock argues that traditional organizational forms can no longer work because organizations have become too complex, advocating a new organizational form that he calls "chaordic", or simultaneously chaotic and orderly. He credits the worldwide success of VISA with its chaordic structure - it is owned by its member banks that both compete with each other for customers and must cooperate by honouring one another's transactions across borders and currencies.

In the chaordic zone we can see the transition from order to chaos, and also the emergence of order out of chaos. This is the "edge of chaos" where new complex systems emerge, whether they are biological, cultural or economic systems. This is also where disruptive and breakthrough innovations and transformations happen, as old institutions and organisations are no longer able to address the existential problems generated by the emerging levels of complexity in the dominant socio-economic design and its unintended side-effects.

Each Era is driven by a dominant socio-economic design that defines the taken for granted assumptions about "the way things are" and "the way things are done around here". For example, in *traditional* Era 1, it is assumed that one's primary loyalty is to the extended family and local "tribe" in a community, and ways of making a living are closer to nature with farming, fishing and forestry, or a dominant industry in the local community such as mining or raw material processing. Small to medium sized towns and rural areas generally retain this dominant socio-economic design even if they are linked into a larger Era 2 or 3 system, through a mall, warehouses or a light industrial zone.

In *modern city/nation centric* Era 2 the dominant socio-economic design is shaped by the organs of the city and the nation state, with local and national small and medium sized enterprises in the majority, while in Era 3 global corporations, digital platforms and regional/global governance and civil society shape the dominant design that makes this system viable.

The dominant design of Era 3 *post-modern global capitalism* peaked in the 1990's, and is increasingly showing its age. The wealthiest 10% in the Era 3 system are now mainly focused on accumulating and conserving their capital, at the cost of decreasing the system's resilience to disruptions. While the wealth of the top 10% may have enabled them to capture entire states and systems of governance even in "democratic systems", it is evident that this is failing to prevent a period of creative destruction whereby previously accumulated capital is released for new purposes.

We are now in this "chaordic zone" in the final stages of Era 3, where a new order (Era 4) is slowly emerging out of the chaos of the collapse of the old. This is a time of innovation and reorganisation, which loosens the rigidity of the dominant institutions such as giant financial institutions, corporations and governance Empires and creates spaces for the new to emerge.

We are at a unique historical moment where globally interconnected collaborative and social media platforms are energising the momentous leap, which is made possible by the new connections emerging from the interactions on such platforms. Such interactions are also driving accelerated learning and innovations so that this will be the fastest leap in history.

Given the global and local challenges we face, including climate change, mass migrations, pandemics and economic collapse, this is perhaps just as well. The question is: will Era 4 engage and scale fast enough to ensure we make it through into the 22nd century as a species?

PART 3: ESSENTIAL ELEMENTS IN LEAPING TO A THRIVING FUTURE

11. Second-Order Change: Is There a Singularity Near You?

We are living in a leap characterised by exponential technologies struggling to interface with mostly linear humans. Advocates of exponential technologies and entrepreneurs believe that they will solve all our problems. Peter Diamandis, founder of the X-Prize and Singularity University in Silicon Valley is but one of many thousands of _technophiles_ that believe science and technology will be our salvation.

Entrepreneurs everywhere are accessing, adopting, and experimenting with exponential technologies, whose performance relative to cost and size is more than doubling every 12 to 18 months. Exponentials, which include technologies such as 3D printing, artificial intelligence, blockchain, advanced robotics, virtual and augmented reality, alternative energy systems, biotechnology, and digital medicine, are sparking a renaissance of innovation, invention, and discovery.

Due to the speed at which exponential technologies are accelerating, some believers in "the singularity" believe we are nearing a point where humans will transform themselves into cyborgs, and download themselves into machines, thereby demonstrating a serious lack of understanding of what it means to actually be human, or even trans-human.

After 40 years and trillions of dollars of investment, artificial intelligence is now actually becoming very good at specific narrowly defined tasks, such as translation, voice recognition, playing certain games, searching the web, doing highly specialised research, animating robots and delivering medical diagnoses. It has not yet succeeded in becoming conscious, nor is it likely to. Abstract reasoning, emotion, and caring for and connecting with others is not on the cards, along with being alive, procreating and experiencing joy or sadness.

While it is good that we have powerful technologies at our disposal to make the world a better place, we also need to ensure that such technologies are used to help us thrive and not simply survive in an unjust system where a few owners of these technologies and platforms extract most of the wealth in the system at the expense of everyone else.

Another concern is that we humans also have a track record of using new technologies in evil, often military ways, whether they be nuclear weapons or killer drones. In other words, our new powers need to be regulated by socially responsible, ethical beings that care about truth, peace, beauty, goodness and justice.

Finally, the vast majority of our species is inherently conservative- we take time to adopt new technologies. Any system, from individuals to organisations and societies, is able to change in two ways: (1) Individual parameters change in a continuous manner but the structure of the system does not alter; this is known as "first-order change." (2) The system changes qualitatively and in a discontinuous manner; this is known as "second-order change." Most people prefer first order change, where things are more predictable and orderly for them.

When exponential technologies meet first order change mindsets and behaviours, what is known as "resistance to change" inserts a great deal of friction and inertia into changing any system. Those already engaged in the momentous leap are open to change and welcome transformational, qualitative change that creates more thriveable outcomes for all stakeholders, making the old dominant design obsolete. Learning how to midwife and catalyse such second-order change processes is a vital skill for all those navigating the chaordic zone in the latest, greatest movement in the human symphony.

12. The Role of Leadership in the Leap

It is popular today to assert that leadership is an outdated concept now that we have reached the "golden age" of self-managing teams and self-organising organisations. This backlash against authority is understandable and even healthy, especially given the toxic nature of many of the dominance hierarchies that still abound on our planet. Authority must be legitimate, and all authority must be questioned regarding its goodness, fairness and care for all stakeholders in the system where that authority is exercised.

Historically, the concept of leadership is essentially non-hierarchical. In contrast to "Command and Control", leadership is a practice of individuals who would be of service to their communities, organisations and the wider world. In any natural system one finds co-opetitive, natural hierarchies where there are many peer-to-peer and predator-prey relationships, which in turn support the health and balance of the whole ecosystem, having evolved over many millennia.

We humans have now evolved to a point where predator-prey relationships within our own species are outlawed, even though the strong may still dominate the weak in many places, and the race is often to the swiftest, so that he who dies with the most toys "wins". In the transition from the hurly-burly of the modern city/nation centric Era 2 and post-modern global capitalism Era 3, to more collaborative, world-centric forms of capitalism in Era 4, integrated forms of leadership are critical.

There are six very different kinds of values driving what leaders can see, feel and do. Rising above the self-interested opportunists, and the diplomats seeking to maintain the conventional order, we find expert achievers in two-thirds of the C-suites. In order to accelerate radical innovation and trigger transformation in time, we need to swell the ranks of integrated leaders, known in psychological assessments as "individualists", "strategists" and "alchemists". The ability to see the whole system from a helicopter perspective and to integrate bigger and more complex chunks of reality rises with each developmental level.

Integrated leadership begins with a deep insight into the values and visions that engage our imaginations with desirable outcomes. This helps inform our priorities, and build thriving, ethical cultures that make good happen.

Leadership does this through motivating people to live fulfilling lives and engage with their purpose and passion at work, within a multi-capital, science based approach that leads to healthy economic growth focused on generating true future value. Circular manufacturing and mobility, resilient habitats and a flourishing biosphere are some of the means to those ends.

This momentous leap is by its very nature a systemic, second-order change. Integrated leadership unlocks the potentials of people at all levels of development to generate the pathways to a thriving future so critical to the future of our species and our biosphere. _In a thriveable world, the ability to create true future value is the ultimate measure of goodness, and of good leadership._

Integrated leadership involves a shift in mindset that redefines the good life while generating the consciousness, cultures, business models and systems that enable us to thrive within a one-planet footprint. The role of leaders must be to trigger the transformation of our lifestyles and the institutions that co-produce them. Integrated leadership is the secret ingredient needed to make that transformation a reality. So, what would it mean to redefine the good life?

13. Redefining the Good Life

In order to shift our world out of the slow-death spiral of the unsustainable models of modern city/nation centric Era 2 and post-modern global capitalism Era 3, we need to redefine the "good life". What would a good life that enabled all forms of life to thrive and evolve into their highest possible selves, look like? The answers to this question are now visible on the horizon, though they take different shapes depending where you are on our exquisitely bountiful planet, and what kinds of business or profession/vocation you are in.

Whatever the outcomes, the process of redefining the good life and making good things happen is being catalysed by integrated leaders midwifing the momentous leap toward collaborative, world-centric forms of capitalism in Era 4.

Redefining the Good Life requires systemic, second-order change, catalysed by integrated leadership. There are three criteria for any project or initiative that seeks to reinvent the good life to enable all forms of life to thrive and evolve into their highest possible selves:

- Firstly, IS IT SYNERGISTIC? Can you identify synergies between your project/ initiative/ organisation and adjacent opportunities and stakeholders/players?

- Secondly, IS IT TRANSFORMATIVE? Assess your organisation's strengths and weaknesses regarding the six key capabilities for transformation, set out below;

- Thirdly, IS IT THRIVEABLE? Map where you are on your journey to good. How can your products, services and processes leapfrog and be reinvented to be better, good, or even very good?

In order to integrate thriveable new ways of doing things into our lives and our organisations, we need six core capabilities for transformation to be woven together into a coherent whole by integrated leadership:

- SEE - cultivate a sense of purpose that embraces multiple horizons that lead to viable futures, so that each stakeholder feels a sense of ownership of that higher purpose;
- FEEL - engage emotion and trigger positive motivation through integrated leadership, motivating people to live fulfilling lives and engage with their purpose at work;
- TOUCH – develop the ability to build multi-stakeholder coalitions to get things done;
- MEASURE – design and integrate systems within a multi-capital, science based approach that leads to healthy, true future value generating growth;
- REINVENT – focus on and build your capabilities to reinvent products, processes, organisations, businesses and entire ecosystems;
- SCALE - nourish the ability to scale what works, while gaining insight into what needs to be done

differently in scaling incremental versus radical/transformative innovations.

Integrated leadership is the science and art of weaving this all together into a whole much greater than the sum of its parts. In my sixth book, "Making Good Happen- Pathways to a Thriving Future", I describe the next steps in this journey, which relies on our ability as a global community to redefine leadership and economics from a thriveable perspective. Integrative maps such as the Good Cube can help you lead yourself and others toward a more thriveable world. Let's explore how the first dimension of the Good Cube, Pathways to Thriving, can act as a first step to plot your course to make the momentous leap a reality.

14. Pathways to Thriving – Embedding the Leap

In order to move beyond incremental to synergistic and systemic innovation in most of our large organisations, cities and socio-economic systems, we need a better map and operating system for transformation. The first dimension in this map comprises the pathways to thriving, which are realistic, measurable innovation pathways that are already open and being invested in right now.

The six pathways to a thriving future are:

1. Values and Visions.
2. Human Development.
3. Thriveable Economies.

4. A Flourishing Biosphere.

5. Resilient Habitats.

6. Circular Manufacturing and Mobility.

These pathways to a thriveable future are related to each other *in a causal sequence that generates the synergies we need for breakthrough innovations* that fuel the momentous leap.

Being able to harness the human energies and flows of ideas, aspirations and capabilities generated in Pathways One (*Values and Visions- Social Capital*) and Two (*Human Development- Human Capital*) in thriveable ways, requires the next generation of governance, economics and finance platforms in Pathway Three (*Thriveable Economies- Financial Capital*) to be able to embed True Future Value into the emerging global system.

Connecting up pockets of the future in the present through the coalesced authority, power and influence of the innovators and visionaries emerging in our organisations and institutions enables rapid scaling and embedding of the most appropriate solutions wherever they "pop" into existence.

This then provides the muscle and intelligence required to empower and accelerate the regeneration of our natural, infrastructure and manufactured capitals so as to create thriveable habitats for all the world's people by 2050 through Pathways Four (*A Flourishing Biosphere- Natural Capital*), Five (*Resilient Habitats- Infrastructure Capital*) and Six (*Circular Manufacturing and Mobility- Manufactured Capital*).

The *"Future Glue"* that integrates all six capitals into social and business models that lead to a regenerative, distributive world-system, comprises *Relationship and Intellectual/Knowledge Capitals*. Through the trust we build through our networks of relationships, and the ideas and initiatives we co-generate, we make good happen and shift our world and ourselves into a more thriveable future through synergistic innovations.

This combination of synergistic innovations and transitions is not entirely predictable in detail, but can be visualised in broad outline through scenarios and engaging with those stakeholders making it happen through approaches such as participative narrative inquiries. The innovation pathways embedded into Pathways One through Six also provide a set of reasonably confident trajectories that enable longer term investments to be made with some degree of assurance, despite the swings and roundabouts of short and medium term fluctuations in the markets.

15. We are the Creators of the Future – Why Not JFDI?

You may have noticed that the first three of the pathways to a thriving future are all a function of human being, learning/adaptation and design/creation: Values and Visions; Human Development and Thriveable Economies. We are the creators of the future.

We live in an age called the "Anthropocene", which literally means the geological era dominated by humans. We have developed god-like powers to alter the biosphere and life conditions on our planet, but sadly it turns out we are not very responsible or caring gods. That is the bad news, along with climate change, pollution, mass extinctions, soil and ocean degeneration, and mega-droughts/floods/storms, all being generated by the excesses of Eras 1-3 and their dominant design assumptions that humans are masters of all they survey, and that we can grow our populations and the economy forever on a planet with finite resources.

The good news is that we also have the power to change our dominant socio-economic designs from degenerative to regenerative, given that the harm we are currently doing is entirely of our own design and making. We can turn this situation around fast, if we will it so.

The last three of the six pathways to a thriving future are all products of human design and co-creation: A Flourishing Biosphere; Resilient Habitats; Circular Manufacturing and Mobility. In other words as long as we have the ever renewable resource of political will to create a thriving future, the design and co-creation of a flourishing biosphere, resilient habitats and circular manufacturing and mobility are not only totally doable by 2050- they are also already advanced in many places on earth. "All" we need to do is ensure they are spread more evenly across the face of our planet.

And Aye, there's the rub. While perhaps 10% of the global population are close to living within a one-planet footprint, the other 90% are a long way from achieving that goal. Given that we are in the midst of a momentous leap in human consciousness, culture, behaviour and socio-economic systems design, we should theoretically be able to get everyone on board with the program of ensuring a thriving future for us all. Not so fast.

But did not 195 countries sign the Paris Climate Agreement in 2015, agreeing to limit global warming to less than two degrees Celsius? Had not 172 countries already ratified the agreement, and begun implementing their commitments by the end of 2017 - apart from the world's second largest carbon emitter, the USA? (Even Syria and N Korea have now signed).

This would be a very short book if all we had to do now was implement the current and emerging technology we already have in place to "JFDI"- (Just Do It – with an F word inserted for emphasis and urgency), to keep warming to below two degrees Celsius.

Creating the Future involves much more than just knowing what new habits, gadgets or technologies to implement - mindsets, culture, behaviours and socio-economic systems need to be reshaped into new forms that are more functional for the new era that is emerging, while avoiding the exit turbulence of the old era that is being transcended and shifted by the new.

The starting point from an individual perspective is learning to see beyond the current challenges to new horizons of possibility- whether renewable energy sources, ways of designing resilient habitats, or reinventing fit for purpose organisations and governance systems. For this to happen individual mindsets have to shift into healthier modes that enable new levels of complexity to be navigated and resolved. As we move from Era 3 to Era 4 in our planetary operating system, we must learn to transcend chaos and complexity.

PART 4: SHAPING THE LEAP THROUGH INTEGRATED LEADERSHIP

16. Integrated Leadership: Transcending Chaos & Complexity

The hallmark of integrated leadership is its ability to synthesise the simplicity the other side of chaos and complexity. Historically, great leadership has always been able to resolve a pattern within apparent chaos and complexity, contrary to the popular myth that we live in a world that is uniquely Volatile, Uncertain, Complex and Ambiguous (known as "VUCA"), and therefore difficult or even impossible to fathom.

Integrated leadership can be exhibited by individuals as well as groups, organisations and networks of people- individual plus collective learning processes are most often both at play in the exercise of the intelligences that enable us to see the simplicity the other side of complexity.

The reality is that certain kinds of minds are able to discern patterns of events and trends in what appear to be chaotic or highly complex situations to most other people. This ability to discern patterns and form appropriate strategies in response, lies at the core of integrated leadership. Integrated leaders can be found at many levels in any organization or system, not just amongst the most powerful or the "top" management team.

Integrated leaders are able to transcend the apparently random or "VUCAlike" conditions they find themselves in- like a good detective, they will sense, probe and experiment with different theories or frames to get to the bottom of what is actually going on. They are also able to cut through confusion, smokescreens, provocations and misinformation with these methods.

We can estimate the ratio of complexity of the mindset of the leader/s dealing with a situation, divided by the complexity of any situation. If that ratio is greater than one, then the leader/s will be able to deal effectively with that situation. They may even have the opportunity to shape the outcomes rather than simply adapting or reacting to the situation.

If that ratio is less than one, then the leader/s will struggle to cope with the situation. They will frequently attempt to label the situation in one of their mental filing cabinet categories. If the situation is genuinely chaotic or complex, this usually leads to poor decision-making and often a great deal of harm. We call this ratio the *"Effective Coherence Ratio"*.

This means that when the world changes, integrated leadership is able to shape outcomes in its favour, as the Effective Coherence Ratio ("ECR") is greater than one. Where the ECR is less than one, and the situation is complex or chaotic, leadership as usual finds itself running out of time with a decreasing number of options, resulting in poor outcomes for some or all stakeholders. Struggling and suffering replace thriving when the ECR ratio is less than one.

When this insight is translated into the world of jobs/tasks and teams, we can speak of the "Size of Person" being greater or less than the "Size of Role". Again, if the ratio of the "SOP"/"SOR" is greater than one, then the leader/worker will be able to deal effectively with that role, and vice versa if the "SOP"/"SOR" is less than one. When scaled up to an entire organization, industry, business ecosystem or society, the same principles apply. Organisational and social learning are key to maintaining relevance and fitness at all levels.

This is why it is essential to assess the complexity handling capabilities of the values, mindsets and cultures of the leadership involved in managing any change or transformation, in order to ensure they are able to effectively deliver thriveable outcomes. Our ability to survive and thrive in the momentous leap we are in depends on this.

17. Shapers, Adapters & Reacters

The highest leverage point in a human activity system resides in the _shared mindsets_ people use to develop their visions, goals and collective actions. When those mindsets shift, the _rules and incentives_ that enable structural change can shift. Underlying shared mindsets we find value systems and cultures that are deeply rooted in one of the four Eras and the three transitions between them.

Do not attempt to meddle with changes in rules and incentives without considering the way in which value systems, cultures and mindsets align, clash and shift. We must design our governance systems, organisations, economic and socio-technical systems to ensure that the momentous leap results in a thriveable future for all, rather than collapse.

Attempting to impose changes in taxation, regulation, legislation, organisational and sociotechnical systems without a prior understanding and evaluation of how our natural human energy and priorities can help or hinder such changes, is one of the chief causes of the mess we are in. The world is weary with the attempts by successive governments and management teams simply trying to squeeze more out of the same old systems everywhere we look. There really are massive limits to growth, and we have hit them hard in the 21st century.

To understand how value systems, cultures and mindsets align, clash and shift, we must consider both their exteriors and interiors. From an *interior* perspective, we can assess mindsets, values and cultures through their _internal conversations and shifting priorities_ or "dominant discourses".

From an *exterior* perspective, we can also observe behaviours and the socio-technical system in focus, watching how an individual or a _social system reacts, adapts to or shapes its environment._ In any major leap between eras, we find three kinds of responses:

- **Shapers** – shapers tend to take the long view and are interested in understanding the complexity of the transitions they are in, so that they may better shape more desirable outcomes. Shapers will tend to be the most innovative and disruptive group in a society and are usually plugged in to global events and curious to know the consequences of these events and trends for their own socio-economic systems and future. Shapers are usually politically progressive and support policies that can catalyse the new era to emerge faster than it otherwise would;

- **Adapters** – adapters are aware of the changes going on around them, and look for opportunities to exploit in the transition they are in. Adapters are pragmatists, and while they might not fully understand the deeper shifts and trends driving the transitions, they are well-equipped to use their existing power and influence to profit from them. Adapters tend to be political moderates, and will shift allegiances based on their interests;

- **Reacters** – reacters are either ignorant of or overwhelmed by the changes around them and tend react emotionally to a major leap by either denying it and continuing with life-as-usual, or attempting to discredit it through their choice of politicians and media. "Conservatives" do exactly what their name suggests: they attempt to keep things the way they were, which is where they feel comfortable. Unfortunately, the world always moves on, and they end up caught in exit turbulence as their old ways collapse around them. They then blame this on elites or foreigners and immigrants and elect populist politicians who promise them "stability" and "order".

18. To Leap is to Integrate & Resonate

When shapers shape, and adapters adapt, a natural developmental process that is part and parcel of growing up is enabling them to mature into responsible adults with foresight, creativity and worldcentric care for the wider world beyond their immediate community and country. They see the gaps between where their world is now, and where it needs to be for more people and life in general to thrive and are able to develop plans and take action to close those gaps in effective, thriveable ways that do not cost the planet.

The leap from cultural creative and progressive modernist to integrated actor and leader, involves a transformation in the way people see the world, their place in it and their own larger purpose. They ask: "Is this all there is?" even if they are wildly successful in what they are doing and feel a pull from the future to take their game to the next level. Their old ways of being and doing no longer satisfy them, or provide the meaning they seek, so they set out on a new quest for the bigger picture, where they must integrate their worldview and their way of being and operating.

There are two different aspects to development. The first is a horizontal movement, where one can expand one's range of operating at a specific level of development by expanding one's cultural and professional horizons. One can explore new cultures, languages, countries or professional options, for example. This involves adding new modules to our existing way of being and doing, without changing our values or priorities, though such new experiences can be a significant catalyst for the second kind of development- vertical development.

Vertical Development refers to advancement in a person's ability to handle complexity and achieve effective coherence and competence. The outcome of vertical stage development is the ability to think in more complex, systemic, strategic, and interdependent ways. It is about what you value, how you think and what you prioritise, which is measured through a wide range of stage development interviews and surveys.

We touched briefly on the first six developmental levels in section 12 above. These first six levels are known as "first-tier" stages of development, which range from egocentric, to ethnocentric to worldcentric, which correspond to the centres of gravity of Eras 1, 2 and 3 outlined in section 8 above. Each of these stages of development believes that their own particular worldview is correct, and that other ways of viewing the world are simply misguided or plain wrong.

When we reach the seventh and eight stages of development at the leading edge of Era 4, we find for the first time the ability to see that all the other perspectives exist and are valid for those operating at those particular stages of development, and to be respected. Integrated leadership recognises that it must resonate with people at all levels of development in all Eras in order to shift mindsets to redefine the good life while generating the consciousness, cultures, business models and systems that enable us all to thrive within a one-planet footprint.

Each level of development and era has its own language, hot buttons, cold buttons and priorities which need to be understood, respected and worked with in any transformation process. By transcending inclusively, integrating synergistically and resonating coherently, integrated leaders become the alchemists our planet needs to transform itself into a flourishing and thriveable world where all life comes fully and joyously alive.

19. From Conflict & Compromise to Synergy

Since the beginning of time our universe has been producing ever more complex, conscious entities and beings including ourselves, through fusion, synergy and synthesis. As a result, we find an ever more diverse range of beings, experiences and extremes arising from those basic physical, chemical, biological and psychological processes of evolution.

Conflict, compromise and synergy are built-in features of such diversity, yet also transformations of each other. Ecosystems evolve in nature through the balancing of these three primeval forces, as they convert the energy around them into forms and functions in a complex web of life.

As we evolve up the ladder of being, we find three things: the first, that the tension between the range of opposites in our lives and societies widens dramatically and often painfully; the second, that the better informed and more intelligent we are, the more humble we have to become about our ability to live meaningful lives and to change anything, even ourselves; and consequently, thirdly, that the cost of gaining the simplicity the other side of complexity can rise very steeply if we do not align ourselves and our lives well in synergistic ways.

While opposites attract and produce interesting new properties and capabilities when they combine, they also create tensions at each new level of being. Nature resolves most of these tensions through the laws of physics, chemistry and biology, and the outcomes are, as we increasingly and happily discover, rather predictable. But when we get to psychology, economics, culture and social affairs, we find that things are rather more chaordic and unpredictable.

There are three ways tensions between opposites can be resolved so that the energy underlying them is released. Conflict is the most obvious way this happens, because its sources and outcomes are generally more dramatic and sudden than the other two. Conflict is so damaging that we have developed entire systems of law and governance to regulate it, at all levels from disputes between neighbours to disputes between superpowers. At the economic level, we regulate competition, and try to create "level playing fields" which are fair to all competitors.

We also release many of our primitive competitive urges through sports and competitions of all kinds.

So, if conflict is the most talked about form of the resolution of the tension between opposites, then the second most talked about way of channelling the energies underlying the tension, is compromise. Sadly, compromise is a weak and unstable form of resolution, as every badly written peace treaty or unhappy and temporary truce between sparring siblings or spouses, will attest.

Compromise usually develops as a result of a desire on the part of two or more parties to avoid conflict, or to "get along" and damp down conflict when the respective parties run out of energy for a fight. Like political candidates smilingly shaking hands with each other after a rancorous debate, outcomes in the compromise zone can only ever aspire to be a temporary truce between opposites, enabling them to sit uneasily alongside each other until the next shock or opportunity arises that sets them off again like firecrackers at a Chinese New Year's celebration. Compromises take much energy to enforce, and when the lid is taken off the pressure cooker, the steam will inevitably blow off.

By activating our capacities for learning, empathy and creativity, we can, instead, craft outcomes in the Synergy Zone.

20. Synergy: The Heart of Creation and Thriving

Synergy = The interaction or co-operation of two or more entities to produce a desirable combined effect greater than the sum of their separate effects.

If we wish to avoid destructive conflict or temporary, unstable compromises, what are the alternatives? Let me introduce you to the Synergy Zone. Nature is built on and through synergies. In fact, anything that is enduring or sustainable is almost by definition, synergistic. We would not be here if it were not for synergies between opposites. Synergies can be very simple or incredibly complex. They come in all sizes. They are everywhere one can detect a pulse. In short, they are the least understood and most important aspect of our existence.

Let's begin with simple synergies. As every English child knows, Jack Sprat could eat no fat, his wife could eat no lean, so betwixt the two of them, they licked the platter clean. This is a nice example of a complementary synergy, where two opposites are more effective with resources than they would be on their own, where each of them would have left half a meal on the table.

Ecosystems in nature and business work better when there are complementary synergies between species and firms. For example, one firm's waste becomes the food for another. Landfills of rubbish that produce the toxic greenhouse gas methane, can sell their waste (methane) to nearby businesses that need cheap energy. No wasted methane and less global warming!

In nature, every species finds a specific niche that enables it to exploit very specific foods and environments without generating too much competition with other species. Even carnivores such as lions will generally only eat the weakest or sickest animals in a herd, and only when they are very hungry. Nature does not waste a single molecule.

Every child knows that birds and bees are attracted to flowers by the nectar each flower offers the pollinators. They also know that big fish eat little fish, and that big fleas have little fleas to bite them, and little fleas have lesser fleas and so ad in infinitum. Leaves, animal faeces and other dead organic matter become compost and nourish the soil. And so it goes for the hundreds of millions of species on our planet.

Yet in our human world, we still have a long way to go to embed this level of graceful efficiency into our social and economic systems. Despite more than fourty years of environmentalism, we are still pumping unprecedented amounts of pollution into our ecosystems. As architect Bill McDonough, the co-inventor of the "Cradle to Cradle" approach to sustainability and design points out, we need to begin thinking about redesigning our industrial and social systems so that one systems waste is another systems food. This trend is growing rapidly as companies seek to save money, energy and resources in their attempts to create a circular (and highly synergistic) economy.

It is because our species has spent enough productive time in the synergy zone that we are still here. If we allowed conflicts and compromises to dominate our existence, we would be caught up in a never-ending game of tit for tat, and medieval revenge dramas writ large at all levels of our society. We see these non-synergistic ways of being in gangs, military conflicts, lawsuits, political campaigns and compromises, divorces, company breakups and mental breakdowns. The only alternative to breakdowns, are breakthroughs.

PART 5: BREAKOUTS, BREAKTHROUGHS & BREAKDOWNS

21. 2.5 Billion Heartbeats of Life & Being Alive

Biologists have calculated that, on average, every mammal dies after 1.5 billion heart beats. What makes the difference is the frequency of heartbeat. An elephant only needs 30 beats per minute; a mouse 1,500; a healthy human 60-70 beats per minute. We homo sapiens are the most astonishing example of what a difference synergistic innovations can make to our longevity.

Thanks to the breakthroughs in our sociotechnical arrangements, we live longer today than ever before; in fact, we have gained a billion heartbeats over our fellow mammals in our lifespan, and our longest-lived members live twice as long as our nearest genetic relative, the chimpanzee.

As the most imperfectly adapted species on the planet, innovation has literally been the lifeblood of our progression from hunter gatherers in the Holocene to planet shapers in the Anthropocene, driven by over *10 000 life-changing and synergistic innovations* in as many years.

Breakdowns often catalyse breakthroughs. While doing what you have always done, you are likely to get what you have always got. When things no longer work, necessity becomes the mother of invention. We have now turned this insight into a professional practice: scientists, researchers, artists, business people, sports people, technologists, engineers, writers and philosophers (amongst many others), have learned to break things down to find out how to make breakthroughs, using the experimental method, summarised as "Fail fast, fail often, fail forward".

For newcomers to this approach, it is important to add: "And do this in a safe practice space where no harm can come to you or others". In other words, do this in the lab, research community or on a practice field, to test your new idea/theory or to perfect whatever new mindset, behaviour, technology, system or approach you are developing.

Without most of us realising it, our species has been creating habitats for the evolution of human potential since the dawn of time, changing what it means to be human in fundamental ways. This is particularly true at this time of the momentous leap, as our entire species becomes interconnected and increasingly interwoven, breaking down old barriers between each other and within ourselves.

Having gained over a billion heartbeats over our fellow mammals in the past 100 000 years or so through our inventive sociality and collaboration, we have given ourselves time to think, empathise, reflect, learn, create, care and connect across the generations and across cultures.

It is, however, critical to be able to distinguish between a breakdown that is part of a larger collapse, from a breakdown that is recoverable and from which an important lesson or breakthrough can be harvested. Sometimes it is wiser to leave a sinking ship and man the lifeboats, than it is to be a hero and go down with the ship. Not all breakdowns and failures result in breakthroughs.

To be able to discern the difference between an irretrievable breakdown and a temporary inconvenience that might result in a learning opportunity, one must be able to see the bigger picture of which the breakdown you are experiencing is a part. This is where the ability to see the patterns of growth, living, maintenance and death experienced by all living systems is key. While keeping our eyes on the prize of breakthroughs and living flourishing lives in a thriveable world, we need to stay alive to the reality of the circles of life.

22. The Circle(s) of Life

Human beings are unique on earth for having four circles of life: biological, psychological, sociological and technological. As a part of nature, we are conceived and born like all other animals. Once we are born into Eras 2, 3 and 4, however, our biological lifecycle becomes intertwined with the psychological, sociological and technological lifecycles prevalent in the specific world in which we take our first breath.

In the biological world, all living beings burn energy to perform three essential tasks: growing, living and repairing wear and tear. Over time, more things break, which means, the repair function consumes more and more energy and when the organism fails to keep up, it dies. The very same process operates in our communities, organisations and civilisations: Grow-Live-Maintain-Die.

Our psychological lifecycle is driven by our personal developmental process, which in turn is enabled or constrained by our life conditions. Normally our biological and psychological lifecycles are synchronised, so that our stages of psychological development mirror our stages of biological development through infancy, toddler, child, teenager, young adult and mature adult. Even as we stop growing biologically, however, we can continue to grow psychologically for the rest of our lives if we so desire.

The sociological lifecycle is much more complex, as it comprises different kinds of social entities growing and developing at very different rates. Families, groups, teams, communities, organisations, large institutions and entire global business ecosystems all have their own distinct lifecycles, which can vary from years to centuries. The oldest organization in the world is the Catholic Church, with a 2 000-year history. Families and communities can trace their histories back many generations, while some global corporations are only a decade old, such as Facebook. Groups and teams are often evanescent, lasting months or years at the most.

Very complex trends and forces in science, society, business and culture drive technological lifecycles. The lifecycle of the average personal computer or mobile phone may be less than two years, while the lifecycle of very large systems and infrastructure from battleships to bridges and dams may be from fifty to five hundred years. The Romans built aqueducts two millennia ago that still function today!

The complexity and uncertainty in modern life is driven by the multiple, often-unpredictable interactions between these four lifecycles. As one peaks, another may hit rock bottom, while the other two remain stable. Our lives are a complex interweaving of personal, family, organisational and social forces and trends that need to be aligned in some way, and preferably synergised for the most positive, thriveable outcomes.

As Shakespeare put it: "There is a tide in the affairs of men, which taken at the flood, leads on to fortune. Omitted, all the voyage of their life is bound in shallows and in miseries. On such a full sea are we now afloat."

To be afloat on such a full sea, and taking the tide at its flood, means that we need to be aware of all four lifecycles in our lives and work if we wish to build on the waves of breakthroughs around us. If any one of these lifecycles is omitted, we may find our life bound in the shallows and miseries of breakdowns as the force of a lifecycle at its lowest ebb pulls us under. On the other hand, taking a synchronised peak in two or more lifecycles can lead on to great fortune. To connect multiple peaks and cycles, we need to find "super-saturated" synergy zones.

23. Triggering Breakthroughs in Synergy Zones

Who knows exactly when the first single-celled amoeba began swimming up a glucose gradient with its elegant little tail? Any guesses on the date of the appearance of the first multi-cellular organism- then plants, algae, fungi, sponges, flatworms, grasshoppers, clams, starfish, sharks, fish, snakes, dinosaurs, birds, dogs, cats, monkeys, and us?

What happened every time a new species emerged, out of the hundreds of millions of species that have ever existed? Each new species was a breakthrough that took place in a rich synergy zone, where there was a super-saturated solution of ingredients and conditions that resulted in a new organism never before seen, better adapted to its life conditions than what came before. And often the species that came before that species went extinct, being less well adapted to the new life conditions.

Unconscious evolution is massively fertile in its productions, continuously recycling every speck of dust, chemistry and energy; generating huge variety, then selecting organisms and behaviours that work better in each set of life conditions, then retaining those features that are most successful- tails, fins, wings, legs, arms, eyes, hands and minds, for example.

In the human world of conscious evolution, the ingredients we are playing with are a combination of biological, psychological, sociological and technological components. Several ingredients are needed for synergistic, thriveable outcomes:

- Firstly, a rich, diverse network of people with breakthrough ideas and plans needing an opportunity to mesh them with other complementary ideas and plans to weave a coherent pathway to a shared superordinate goal;

- Secondly, insights into the energetic and mindset dynamics that can empower those on this pathway, as well as the blockages which can stop or disrupt forward movement;

- Thirdly, the ability to align diverse agendas into a synergistic win/win/win desirable outcome which can engage people's imaginations;

- And finally, the ability to navigate the turbulence on the journey along that pathway, and to embed change and transformation deeply into the system, winning minds and hearts, balancing power and love.

And all of this is cycling in the endless stream of lifecycles of Grow-Live-Maintain-Die that operate in our communities, organisations and civilisations. What a complex, marvellous tapestry is woven within and around us every minute of every day, even while everything appears quiet and calm and the surface of reality like a still pond.

Two point five billion heartbeats of life for each of us lucky ones that make it all the way to the "end"; 10 000 life-changing, synergistic innovations that make it possible for us to glide effortlessly over the surface of our earth in amazing contraptions that skim across the water, earth and air. We have so much to grateful for, yet so much more to do. As much as we might like to say: "Stop the ride- I want to get off", evolution cares not for our personal dreams, hopes, frustrations and aspirations.

Yet, as a species, we are gifted with some of the most advanced minds yet discovered, along with generous hearts and sensuous bodies that crave to love and be loved. We might not be able to change life conditions to suit us exactly the way we might wish, but we do have the power to react to, adapt to and even shape what comes next for us. Even the magnificent dolphins, elephants, whales and other large brained mammals would be envious of that fact, if they could.

24. Action and Care Co-evolve

Human evolution seems to be driven by the biological, psychological, social and technological need to balance any living system, at all levels of scale, in a healthy zone between love and power. As we develop as individuals, families, tribes, action groups, social institutions, enterprises, networks and communities toward the moment when we are ready to take a momentous leap in meaning and capability to second tier "being" as opposed to first tier "existence", we find our capacity for care/relationship, together with action/engagement, rising steeply.

This is what we can now observe occurring on a planetary scale amongst a few hundred million people at the forefront of human evolution and thriveable transformation. This is an inherently messy process, with two leaps forward and one leap backward on occasion, as we learn to adapt to and shape the emerging life conditions that present themselves in our emerging global civilization.

Although we will experience many local collapses in dysfunctional communities, societies and socio-political systems, we find that the cathartic if tragic consequences of such collapses actually strengthens the capacity to design and take actions that enhance thriveability, while also deepening the bonding and mutual care between newly emerging global connections.

While at one level we all function as individuals as best we can in this chaordic zone, we find a clarity of meaning and purpose in this evolutionary process, that helps build the trust that is critical to nurturing the global meshworks that can deliver a regenerative, inclusive world civilization.

We then find ourselves reframing our personal and collective accomplishments in ever bigger circles of care and engagement. It is those accomplishments we need to celebrate, communicate and build on, rather than the diverse collapses in worn out authoritarian, exploitative and corrupt ways of being and governing, which have plagued us for so many millennia.

This will not be a utopian outcome, however, as the complexity we generate in the process is challenging, and the ability to find the simplicity the other side of complexity in all of this is a hard won outcome of much struggle within ourselves and between ourselves and others who are often in denial, cynical, enraged or apathetic.

Perhaps the hardest people to work with are those who are experiencing an ego boost from their unearned "accomplishments" in hoarding wealth and maintaining the existing dysfunctional systems, and those who are deeply frozen in fear. Without conceding an inch to their pretensions and blockages, we must still include them in our circle of care as we hospice those parts of our world that are slowly dying and being replaced by more thriveable solutions to humanity's challenges.

Just look around you and notice the sheer diversity, sumptuousness and glory of the world around you. Beneath the jaded exteriors of cynical city commuters, the calloused hands of those toiling the soil in the lands and seas that feed us, the glossy surfaces of the endless parade of celebrities and wannabe celebrities and those feeding us fashion; inside every one of those hearts and minds lies an uncharted territory of possibilities waiting to be revealed and expressed, brought to life in the world.

We live in an era ripe with opportunities for breakthroughs; breakthroughs that can and are catalysing a momentous leap for our species: a new movement in the symphony of human history.

25. Breaking Out is not Breakthrough

In a perfect world we all desire to be free of external constraints and to live our lives as we see fit, according to our own values, as long as we also respect the rights of others. We also all desire some measure of economic empowerment to make a living and live a better life, even a "good" life.

When we talk about breakthroughs and breakdowns, we need to context these within the relationships of power and love, action and care, which are often balanced on a knife-edge in conditions of rapid change and social upheaval. This is why there is a non-linear relationship between the events that trigger a cataclysmic shift, and the sheer scale of the social consequences that result.

Roughly half of humanity currently lives in authoritarian societies where there is limited or no freedom of expression. The other half live in societies that range from partially free and democratic to fully free and democratic. In the authoritarian half of the world, the rulers have a great deal more power than their subjects and use this power to perpetuate the unfair state of affairs that condemns those populations to maintain the unfair status quo. In the freer half of the world, economic inequality is rising except in more enlightened parts of the world such as Scandinavia, so being politically "free" does not necessarily confer economic freedom.

We only need to look at the Arab Spring uprisings together with the wars in Syria and Libya to see how rapidly social powder-kegs can explode as a result of specific events driven by one or more individuals. On 25 January 2011 hundreds of thousands of protesters started to gather in Tahrir Square and planted the seeds of unrest which, days later, finally unseated the incumbent president, Hosni Mubarak, after 30 years of power. Almost a year after Tunisia had erupted in mass demonstrations, the central Cairo protests triggered further waves of change across the Middle East and North Africa, in what became known as the Arab Spring.

While nine out of ten Egyptians and Tunisians responded to a poll that they used Facebook to organize protests and spread awareness, the role of the social networks wasn't central in countries like Syria and Yemen, where there is little Facebook penetration. Statistics show that during the Arab Spring the number of users of social networks, especially

Facebook, rose dramatically in most Arab countries, particularly in those where political uprising took place.

Most approaches to social change and personal transformation operate either on the level of individuals (micro-reductionism) or "society as a whole" (macro-reductionism)[ii]. What has been missing for many decades is an intelligent way to describe and work with social entities on all scales (from sub-individual to transnational) that are best analysed through their components- what one might describe as various "meso-level" descriptions, creations and interventions. For example, households, communities, organisations and organs of governance all operate in different strata in the meso-level space. It is at this meso-level that meaningful, beneficial change can be scaled up from the individual to the social level.

Sadly, breaking out is not the same as breaking through. While environmental and political activism has become a significant force for change in the past century, knowing what you do not want is not the same as knowing what you do want and structuring ways to bring about that desired future. Skilful means are required to make lasting changes in one's own life and that of others. While breaking out may provide a temporary form of relief, it has to be part of a bigger plan that embeds thriveable transformation at many levels, creating new structures and processes that work better for everyone.

PART 6: STILL CENTRES IN SPINNING WORLDS

26. Is it Nobler to Plug or Unplug? Components of Social Change

We now know that reducing change/transformation to either personal (micro) levels, or social (macro) levels, does a grave injustice to those seeking to be more skilful agents of change and transformation. The real action happens in the multiple levels between macro and micro change, at the meso level.

Individuals, households, communities, organisations and organs of governance all operate in different strata at the meso-level, which is where meaningful, beneficial change can be scaled up from the individual to the social level. This is known as an "assemblage approach" to change and transformation, developed by French social theorist and philosopher Manuel DeLanda, following the late French philosopher Giles Deleuze's ideas of difference and repetition, and the need to understand social change as a complex, non-linear, stratified phenomenon.

The relationship between an assemblage and its components is complex and non-linear: assemblages are formed and affected by heterogeneous populations of lower-level assemblages, but may also act back upon these components, imposing restraints on or adaptations in them.

Individuals, households, communities, organisations, organs of governance at regional, national and transnational levels (let's call them "components"), can be characterized along three axes/dimensions:

- **Axis 1 - The Material-Expressive axis** defines the variable roles a component may play- components are self-subsistent and may be "unplugged" from one assemblage and "plugged" into another without losing their identity- this is a critical, empowering capability and choice- whether to "plug in and play the game", or to "unplug and play a different/better game";

If we wish to shape thriveable futures, rather than simply react or adapt to what life conditions impose on us, we must master values and complexity. We have seen that chaos and confusion are always relative to the perspective we apply to a situation. Those with more complex worldviews are able to recognise patterns in apparently random, unpredictable situations, and use those patterns to help shape more thriveable outcomes.

The Momentous Leap Professor Clare Graves described in his 1974 paper to the American Psychological Association, involved the ability to cross a chasm of unbelievable depth of meaning in his research subjects. What exactly did he mean by that mysterious phrase? Graves estimated in 1974 that 1 in 10,000 brains had developed different biological features and frequencies: that these people didn't conform to the norms of society because their minds were wired for a different paradigm.

Following his discovery of the six value systems that evolved through Eras 1, 2 and 3, Graves had stumbled upon human minds that would come to characterise Era 4 thinking and action, which he called "Second Tier" to distinguish it from the "First Tier" or the first six value systems in Eras 1-3. Such

"Second Tier" thinking is characterised by an integrative capability: to understand the bigger picture and recognize that the six value systems in Eras 1-3 are crucially important to the whole and to the evolutionary process.

This seventh level integrative capability is then followed by an eighth level holistic thinking capability which not only understands the bigger picture but is also able to incorporate all of the previous value systems and ways of being and doing, along with the multiple levels of interaction, harmonics and energetic dynamics that are going on below the surface.

Roughly 90% of Earth's population is still operating in First-Tier Thinking in Eras 1-3, where each level and Era is busy trying to convince the others that they are wrong, that they can't see what is happening right in front of their eyes. This is one of the main reasons that we see so much apparent chaos and confusion as these three Eras and six value systems have all been mashed together by globalisation, leading to inevitable conflicts and misunderstandings around the world.

- **Axis 2** - We must accelerate the momentous leap to integrated, second-tier thinking and action if we are to co-create the foundations for a thriving global civilisation by 2050. The **Territorializing-Deterritorializing Axis** highlights processes in which a component is involved-components can and do "colonise" their subjects/customers, whether they are governments or large corporations, big media or big NGO's. There is a continual tension between different kinds of power in the relationships between these entities, in which groups of smaller components can rise up effectively against more powerful components;

- **Axis 3 - The Encoding/Decoding Processes** in which specialized expressive media (genetic/linguistic resources) intervene in "coding"/"decoding" the assemblage.

As an example of an assemblage, consider an ecosystem:

- The **material role** here is performed by the soil, sunlight, trees, animals, etc.
- The **expressive role** is performed by the forms, colours, habits, etc. of the aforementioned components.
- The **territorializing role** would be played by factors such as food chains, adaptive traits, conducive climate and other elements that maintain the components and their relationships and thus the identity and durability of the assemblage.
- The **deterritorializing role** would be played by such factors as climate change, invasion by exotic species, evolutionary mutation and other elements that recombine or replace various components and roles within the assemblage, leading to its dissipation or reformulation.
- A **linguistic/coding role** could be played by an environmental discourse seeking to protect an ecosystem.

We've already seen the way in which the "infinite loops" of panarchic processes can help model the circles of life that result from the interplay of these different roles in human systems. Let's now examine how our values and ability to master complexity can shape thriveable outcomes.

27. Mastering Values & Complexity

In section 16, we explored Integrated Leadership: Transcending Chaos & Complexity, and learned that integrated leaders are able to transcend the apparently random or "VUCAlike" conditions they find themselves in- like a good detective, they will sense, probe and experiment with different theories or frames to get to the bottom of what is actually going on.

In section 17, we discovered that the highest leverage point in a human activity system resides in the _shared mindsets_ people use to develop their visions, goals and collective actions. When those mindsets shift, the _rules and incentives_ that enable structural change can shift. Underlying shared mindsets we find value systems and cultures that are deeply rooted in one of the four Eras and the three transitions between them.

In section 22, we learned that human beings are unique on earth for having four circles of life: biological, psychological, sociological and technological. As a part of nature, we are conceived and born like all other animals. Once we are born into Eras 2, 3 and 4, however, our biological lifecycle becomes intertwined with the psychological, sociological and technological lifecycles prevalent in the specific world in which we take our first breath.

If we wish to shape thriveable futures, rather than simply react or adapt to what life conditions impose on us, we must master values and complexity. We have seen that chaos and confusion are always relative to the perspective we apply to a situation. Those with more complex worldviews are able to recognise patterns in apparently random, unpredictable situations, and use those patterns to help shape more thriveable outcomes.

The Momentous Leap Professor Clare Graves described in his 1974 paper to the American Psychological Association, involved the ability to cross a chasm of unbelievable depth of meaning in his research subjects. What exactly did he mean by that mysterious phrase? Graves estimated in 1974 that 1 in 10,000 brains had developed different biological features and frequencies: that these people didn't conform to the norms of society because their minds were wired for a different paradigm.

Following his discovery of the six value systems that evolved through Eras 1, 2 and 3, Graves had stumbled upon human minds that would come to characterise Era 4 thinking and action, which he called "Second Tier" to distinguish it from the "First Tier" or the first six value systems in Eras 1-3. Such "Second Tier" thinking is characterised by an integrative capability: to understand the bigger picture and recognize that the six value systems in Eras 1-3 are crucially important to the whole and to the evolutionary process.

This seventh level integrative capability is then followed by an eighth level holistic thinking capability which not only understands the bigger picture but is also able to incorporate all of the previous value systems and ways of being and doing, along with the multiple levels of interaction, harmonics and energetic dynamics that are going on below the surface.

Roughly 90% of Earth's population is still operating in First-Tier Thinking in Eras 1-3, where each level and Era is busy trying to convince the others that they are wrong, that they can't see what is happening right in front of their eyes. This is one of the main reasons that we see so much apparent chaos and confusion as these three Eras and six value systems have all been mashed together by globalisation, leading to inevitable conflicts and misunderstandings around the world.

We must accelerate the momentous leap to integrated, second-tier thinking and action if we are to co-create the foundations for a thriving global civilisation by 2050.

28. Connectivism: Accelerated Evolution

In the 21st century, human evolution is accelerating for four principle reasons:

- Access- there is now a much greater availability of resources that can help you get things done;

- Trust- reduces the amount of time and energy spent in completing a transaction;

- Abstraction- means we can minimize the energy required to find, use and mobilize available resources;

- Awareness- enhanced awareness enables us to synthesise vast amounts of information and complexity to co-create thriveable outcomes with less effort and resources.

Ultimately these effects change the thermodynamics of the system. Each has the potential to increase the reaction rate of networks. In social networks, connectivism is the integration of principles explored by chaos, network, and complexity and self-organization theories. Learning is a process that occurs within nebulous environments of shifting core elements not entirely under our control. Learning (defined as actionable knowledge) can reside outside of ourselves (within an organization or a database), is focused on connecting specialized information sets, and the connections that enable us to learn more are more important than our current state of knowing.

Today our every decision is based on rapidly altering foundations. New information is continually being acquired. The ability to draw distinctions between important and unimportant information is vital. The ability to recognize when new information alters the landscape based on decisions made yesterday is also critical.

To accelerate the momentous leap to a thriving Era 4 global civilisation, we must accelerate the reaction rate of our networks to produce thriveable outcomes, and we must do this faster than the speed at which the retrogressive forces of the fossil-fuel owned politicians and corrupt monopolists/oligopolists can retard our progress. This literally is a race for survival, as well as a race to the top rather than a race to the bottom.

The momentous leap to and through second-tier ways of knowing, thinking, relating and doing makes many demands on those who are in that upward flow. It means that our capacity to know, be and do more is more critical than what we currently know, are and do. Not only must we nurture and maintain relationships to facilitate continual learning- we must also enhance our ability to see connections between fields, ideas, and concepts and develop this as a core skill. We must also maintain openness to new information, ideas and connections while being able to follow through on our implementation of projects and plans that are working.

In section 23 we explored the ingredients needed to trigger breakthroughs in synergy zones, and in section 26, the implications of a plug 'n play approach to social change. These two insights share a common root: change and learning come about because we either add a new connection/s to our network; or we can remove an old connection/s; we can also increase or weaken the strength of some of the connections in our network; and we can link our network to other networks that bring fresh perspectives and fruitful collaborations.

We are operating in a turbulent field of social transformation. The ride is guaranteed to be full of shocks and surprises, as well as amazing new opportunities. Staying centred and balanced in the midst of the chaordic zones we are in is essential if we are not to burn out or disintegrate.

29. Staying Centred in Turbulence

"Breathe in slowly, hold for five, breathe out slowly". Perhaps the most soothing words in any language. The calming effects of breath-awareness, mindfulness and meditation are well known and increasingly widely practised, and the benefits well researched. Most people use these mindtools to reduce stress and increase creativity, as exemplified by companies such as Google, who have in-house meditation coaches.

At the level of first-tier consciousness, this is important and helpful. When engaged in the flows that enable second-tier being and doing to crystallise at different levels of scale, however, we can and must take this much further. Philosopher Ken Wilber sums it up neatly when he says:

"If I contract as ego, it appears that I am confined in the body, which is confined in the house, which is confined in the large universe around it. But if I rest as Witness—the vast, open, empty consciousness—it becomes obvious that I am not in the body, the body is in me; I am not in this house, the house is in me; I'm not in the universe, the universe is in me. All of them are arising in the vast, open, empty, pure, luminous Space of primordial Consciousness, right now and right now and forever right now. Therefore, be Consciousness."[iii]

In coaching and psychoanalysis, the perspective Wilber is describing is known as the "third position" or "third". This is where, instead of experiencing a situation from the first position of your own experience and filters, or the second position where you assume the perceptual position of another person, you assume an objective observer position.

In third you see and hear yourself and others outside of you as if on a cinema screen. Third position is useful if when you want to shift from emotionally charged experiences to get an objective view. Third is also useful for stepping back and getting insights into situations and seeing and hearing the bigger picture.

You would assume the third position to get your conscious mind insights after conducting a 'second position' exercise where you have stepped into the strong feelings. Third position has a different type of feelings associated with it than first. Overall, the feelings are more objective and neutral than those experienced in first position. Some people tend to spend a lot of their day in third, and not experiencing the emotions and strong feelings associated with first. Third position is very useful for assuming the role of being your own coach, and essential if you are going get into your strategic psychological helicopter to transcend the problem and transform the mindsets of those responsible for solving it.

Be very clear about the sensations you experience in first and how they support you or perhaps limit you. If you need more objectivity in a given situation, step to an analytical third position. If you are over analysing, step to experiential first. If you would like more empathy with another step to second position and see and hear from another's perspective. If you seek to learn quickly use second position and associate an expert with this perspective. Most importantly increase the number of choices available to you in your life by becoming highly flexible with your use of the triple position.

In section 5, we noted that what pre-eminent management guru Peter Drucker called: "Getting into our strategic psychological helicopter and transcending the problem", has become more in evidence in executive and political corridors of power in the past 50 years or so. This enabled challenges to be viewed from multiple perspectives, producing solutions at emergent levels of thinking that had never been tried before. Now, half a century later, we see hundreds of millions of people getting into their strategic psychological helicopters, including, thankfully, you.

30. Getting Real- From Happiness to Thriving

Taking the momentous leap is a good start to creating a better world. Being a still centre in a spinning world provides a strong base from which you can begin to shape the world around you, rather than simply reacting or adapting. How can we overcome the challenges of the 21st century and benefit from all the opportunities it offers us?

The pursuit of happiness has sadly become the pursuit of comfort, wealth and materialism. Happiness, like the weather, is full of ups and downs, as our emotions and feelings ebb and flow with the roller-coaster ride of life. We must transition to a world where meaning, engagement, positive emotion and accomplishment blend into a satisfying recipe for flourishing, to thrive in the beautiful, connected simplicity the other side of the collapse of our consumerist, hyper-competitive global political economy. We need a race to the top, not a race to the bottom.

In 1972, the Club of Rome issued its "Limits to Growth" Report. The report stated that we will overshoot planetary boundaries in the 21st-century causing a global crisis and possible collapse given delays in responding to this information. Indeed, we have gone from a footprint of one third of a planet in 1700 to a 1.7 planet footprint in 2018. By 2050, if we continue with business as usual, we will need 2.3 planets to supply our species with the basics of life. This is not survivable.

With business as usual we will blow our global carbon budget of 755 gigatonnes ensuring we push past 2°C of warming to a runaway climate change scenario. At our current rate of emissions of 42 gigatonnes output of carbon dioxide greenhouse gases, that gives us 18 years before we must stop emitting greenhouse gases altogether. The 2017 World Economic Forum global risks report places climate change related risks at the very top of the list. Extreme weather events, natural disasters, water and food crises, ecosystem collapse and large-scale migration are just a few of the major risks we face now globally.

Of course, we all desire a thriving future. The growing sustainability gap however, makes this highly problematic. Right now, individuals, societies and organisations are transitioning too slowly from business as usual to more sustainable, even thriveable, ways of operating. This is currently reinforced by perverse incentives that value financial capital returns about everything else. It is this culture and leadership gap where we have the highest leverage to shift mindsets and values.

When people feel under pressure or attack, they simply self-contract, and resist change, no matter how persuasive you think your arguments might be against racism, fundamentalism, or out of control capitalism. Shifting mindsets is delicate work, and we will explore these intricacies in more detail in the next hour. Engaging people's pragmatic imaginations with ideas that can lead to desirable outcomes is key to embedding thriveability. Seed mind thought leaders such as Clare Graves, Buckminster Fuller, Jean Gebser and others have opened the eyes of millions of people- it is now up to us to turn that into many millions who can turn these mindshifts into worldshifts, through capability and culture shifts.

Clusters of innovations enable and embed leaps in human progress. Evolution favours processes & structures that facilitate flows of energy, information and resources, with the most synergistic outcomes of those intermingling flows being translated into embedded innovations that scale species wide. This has already happened three times in our evolution and is now being evidenced in our fourth leap. Let's examine the dynamics of how each of these leaps occurs.

PART 7: CONSCIOUS EVOLUTION

31. A New Model of Human Evolution

What I am proposing here is a new model of human evolution that embraces all four evolutionary modes present in humans and other social animals. This is the core of what I call the "biopsychosociotechno" story, which recapitulates the dynamic interactions between the biological, psychological, sociological and technological forces shaping our future as a species.

Over 3.5 bn years of evolution from single celled organisms to us, the arrow of evolution has swung decisively from unconscious Darwinian evolution to conscious cultural evolution. Despite 5 mass extinctions to date, life has bounced back in ever-greater profusion, and today we find that nurture is as important as nature in defining the future possibilities for our species.

When people gush about how "wonderful" nature is, and how everything should be "natural", remember the killer fly, as well as her ordinary fly relatives. Evolution has meant that the predatory killer fly can see other flies in slow motion so she can eat them- in turn slow flies see our fly swatter in slow motion. Nature is full of predator-prey relationships, where the race is not always to the swiftest, nor the battle to the strongest or smartest, but it pays to bet that way.

This is pure Darwinian evolution- literally survival of the fastest. Most of nature operates on this Darwinian principle, until we get to larger creatures with larger brains, and what we might call self-awareness or consciousness. Then, the advantages of collaboration become paramount, as we see the emergence of collective intelligence everywhere from dolphins to apes to dogs. Homo sapiens "success" as the global top predator (a mixed bag, indeed), is the result of our ability to evolve through post-Darwinian forms of evolution.

In pure **Darwinian** evolution, the individual *organism* is selected- the slow fly, for example. In **Skinnerian** evolution, the individual *behaviour* is selected- Pavlov's dog learns to get food by responding to a bell. In **Popperian** evolution, the individual *hypothesis* is selected- for example, humans have evolved some paranoid tendencies because it paid to think that there might be a lion behind a rock waiting to devour us, rather than casually strolling across the savannah without a care in the world and then- crunch! Corporate and business strategy is all about Popperian evolution, developing the foresight to enable us to create a better future. Sadly, politics remains a largely Darwinian and Skinnerian pursuit.

Today we condition youngsters to become good citizens, and to avoid dangerous risks. Today we develop hypotheses about climate change that tell us we should have a home that is at least 10m above sea level if we wish to have dry feet by 2050. And that we should stop burning fossil fuels…and so on.

In **Gregorian** evolution, the unit of selection is the *group or population that learns and adapts together fastest.* In fact, through our innovations and creativity we are now pre-adapting ourselves to future scenarios. In a learning society we see continuous improvements in the quality of life for all creatures, as well as beneficially disruptive innovations such as digital media and social networks which enable us to share our learning and caring.

The race now is between those with enough foresight, collaborative ability and creativity to shape a thriving future, and those who would pull us back into the dark ages of feudal corporate and political overlords, where the few profit from the hard labour of the many. Our species has gone from Darwinian to Gregorian evolution in a remarkably short time thanks to the rapid evolution of our brain and the adaptive complexity of our social networking and structures. The implications of this model are vast, so I'll stick to ways it can help us catalyse the momentous leap toward thriveable transformation in Era 4.

32. Transition from Era 3 to Era 4

As the most imperfectly adapted species on the planet, innovation has literally been the lifeblood of our progression from hunter gatherers in the Holocene to planet shapers in the Anthropocene, driven by over 10 000 life-changing and synergistic innovations in as many years.

The first, largely European Renaissance gave us the power to eradicate much disease, discomfort, hunger and ignorance through innovations in science, technology, organizations, culture and governance, making us the most prolific top predator in our biosphere- and with the same wand, also gave us the power to eliminate much of life on earth as we know it, either deliberately through weapons of mass destruction, or inadvertently through our sheer numbers and over-consumption.

To make the transition from "less bad" through "sustainable" and "net positive" to "thriveable" involves identifying robust innovation pathways based on principles and metrics which clearly identify how to maximize the thriving of an organization's human and social capital for the least natural and manufactured capital footprint possible. The effective allocation of funds by capital markets to organizations that deliver thriveable innovation by harnessing their intellectual and financial capital to this end would then be much more likely, and the trillions needed to ensure we close the sustainability and sustainable development gaps much better targeted.

In our individualistic, technology obsessed modernist era, social isolation is increasing to epidemic proportions. Harvard professor Robert Putnam provides a wealth of telling statistics in his book Bowling Alone, asserting that "Our growing social-capital deficit threatens educational performance, safe neighbourhoods, equitable tax collection, democratic responsiveness, everyday honesty, and even our health and happiness."

Social capital appears to be the highest form of synergy for us humans, given that we are fundamentally a collaborative, social-learning species. Yet the social capital we found in our Era 1 hunter-gatherer tribal bonds is very different from the social capital we developed in our towns, cities, and Empires in Era 2, which is again very different from the corporate/brand and sports affiliations which characterize much of the social capital we experience in our modernist Era 3.

Chronic illnesses are rising rapidly as a result of Era 3 loneliness, which is often accentuated by the hyper-connectivity of our times as we spend most of our day plugged into our machines and the Internet. To synergise social capital we need to appreciate how it is formed through a mixture of all the other capitals that it is made up of: human, relationship, intellectual, infrastructure, manufactured, natural and financial. And also appreciate how this mélange creates different kinds of value for different kinds of people.

Evolution produces complex, conscious entities and beings, including us, through fusion, synergy and synthesis. This means that we progress through the creation of an ever more diverse range of beings, experiences and extremes which are in turn "synergized" through social and economic systems, sciences and technologies. Value is created when such a synergy enables us to do or experience something that helps us thrive- which is the ultimate function of governance and value-creation systems of all kinds.

33. Era 4 OS: Activated Clusters of Thriveable Entities?

Right now it is difficult to put a name to Era 4. The characteristics of its "operating system" are still emerging, and its success is not guaranteed. What is clear is that Era 4 must ensure that our species and biosphere are thriveable, while transcending and including Eras 1, 2 and 3 such that the healthy aspects of those earlier, yet more fundamental human operating systems are ensured. What might that look like? Building from the bottom-up, we would need to include the healthiest capabilities of our species from Eras 1-3-namely:

<u>Era 1 - Small Teams/Communities based on Family & Tribal Bonds</u> – our ability to collaborate and get things done to ensure our survival and thriving is grounded in what we have learned from millions of years of operating in small hunter-gatherer bands. What we learn today as "teamwork" in world-centric and multi-cultural settings is the same set of skills and values that we have always used to bring families, teams and tribes of workers together. This has always involved creating a common bond based on a shared identity and purpose. Much of what has been written about organisational cultures is derived from this core human operating system. Without this core level of motivation and bonding, not much gets done;

<u>Era 2 - Cities & Empires based on Dominance Hierarchies</u> – as we scaled up from Era 1 to living in towns and cities, full of others who were not related or familiar to us, an overarching form of governance emerged- the City/State/Empire. A set of rules and laws emerges, often bolstered by a monotheistic religion, that creates the basis for civic order and for managing conflicts between diverse groups. New institutions and roles emerge that act to enforce these rules and laws, from rulers to police to courts to lawyers to armies to churches and priests, along with the governance systems of Empires including parliaments and politicians.

These conflicts and their resolutions our still played out vividly in our drama and action movies in every household with a TV or internet connection;

<u>Era 3 - Corporations & Nation States based on Hierarchies and Networks</u> – over the past five centuries the emergence of global trade flows and movements of people and ideas has sparked the longest period of sustained socio-economic growth ever, with all its unintended, often harmful side-effects. As this wave of modernism peaks across our planet, accelerated by digital, biotech, nanotech and green technologies, we also see the reaction of post-modernism and sustainability seeking to limit the harmful effects of Era 3.

The post-modern reaction to Era 3 is, at its most productive, generating a key strand of the emerging Era 4 operating system: thriveability, meaning the capability to enhance thriving within social floors and environmental ceilings. The economics of this shift requires a fractal-like clustering of thriveable entities at all scales (whether communities, small/medium sized businesses, local/ regional/central governments, civil society organisations and/or thought leaders as well as global organisations like the UN and its agencies) that are activated in clusters of networks to deliver thriveable outcomes. The evidence shows that thriveable organisations and investments deliver superior returns, and this is gradually shifting the focus of major investors toward what look like increasingly thriveable investments and organisations.

The outcomes we seek are slowly emerging, initially in a rather unpredictable fashion, from the synthesis and synergies activated by the leaders who "get" the indisputable logic of this new way of operating[iv]. Synergistic-innovations and leanings can and do flow pretty much instantly from any level in this cluster of networks to any other level anywhere on the planet.

34. The BioPsychoSocioTechno Innovation Story

Clusters of interwoven biological, psychological, sociological and technological innovations have literally driven the evolution of our species, and still do. This is what I call the "BioPsychoSocioTechno Story". Think of this story as a chain of causation that works both ways, from the bio to the techno, and vice-versa. Or think of them as four musical notes, which can be played as a chord, with one or more of the notes being dominant depending upon the tune being played.

For example, let's take a simple breakthrough, fire. Before we discovered fire, we had difficult staying warm and getting enough food, because we could not cook and could not huddle around a warm fire together in the dark night. A new technology (TECHNO), fire, suddenly meant cooking could release more nutrients from raw food, giving us more energy (BIO), which also meant we shared meals around the fire, creating stronger bonds between us (PSYCHO), that led to better collaboration between members of the tribe (SOCIO), and ultimately, to more of us surviving those ice ages and dangerous predators.

Fast forward a few hundred thousand years, and we find ourselves spending a great deal of our time in front of the 21st century equivalents of the campfire, whether our digital devices or the local coffee shop or restaurant. We can now bond and collaborate with some of the 1.5 billion people on Facebook or get to know our friends and colleagues better to the sound of the cappuccino machine or the waiter taking our order. Again, the new technologies have biological, psychological, and sociological consequences, which must be taken into account in considering their function, design and operation.

We cannot sustain a momentous leap unless we embed the BioPsychoSocioTechno story into the way we think, design, build and operate our planet. All life on earth depends on nature working well, and for that to happen in the future we need healthy human beings who are psychologically well adjusted. These humans need to get on well together and build trusting, caring relationships that enable them to manage our planet well. As these relationships coalesce into networks of capability, power, authority and influence, they create social capital that enables social institutions to function well and brands to be trusted.

The stability and predictability generated by social capital encourages the production and exchange of intellectual and manufactured capital, adding to the wealth and prosperity of a society. Infrastructure capital then acts to facilitate the processes of production and exchange through resilient habitats plus transport and communications networks that interconnect them. Then, financial capital can play its proper role as a scorecard (unit of value) and medium of exchange, and not the be-all and end-all of our hyper-financialised economy. In business and investment circles, the BioPsychoSocioTechno story is partially recognised as an approach to integrated thinking and management called "multi-capitalism". In the thriveability approach to multi-capitalism, we recognise 8 capitals:

- Biological- natural and human capitals
- Psychological- relationship and intellectual capitals
- Sociological- social and financial capitals
- Technological- manufactured and infrastructure capitals.

Progress in human civilisation is advanced through clusters of innovations that interweave the 8 capitals in synergistic ways, creating more value for more people as a result. To make this value sustainable and thriveable, it needs to be measured as True Future Value.

35. Transcending Era 4 Challenges

The challenges of Era 4 in the 21st century are unprecedented, as are the opportunities. Synergistic-innovations based on breakthrough synergies between natural, human, social and technological capitals have the potential to change what it means to be human in many beneficial ways. Just as Adam Smith struggled to define human nature in 1759, so we are faced with a similar conundrum today. The answers to several key questions could make the difference between the success or failure of our species and biosphere:

- Will the rampant individualism and narcissism inherent in much of the developed world, (and now spreading to the developing world), triumph over the ability of people to bond around common causes and interests to survive and thrive?

- Can the political economies of corrupt nations be reformed in time to ensure wiser policymaking that considers the longer-term implications of key policy decisions so that future generations actually have a future?

- Will the "sharing economy" and the commons movements be destined for the trash heap of history as right-wing fanatics and fascists take over the levers of control in many societies?

- Will renewable energy adoption scale-up fast enough to substitute for fossil fuels by 2050 and keep us within our carbon budget?

- Will the shift in power to Asia enable us to maintain some kind of equilibrium in world order and maintain peace despite climate change induced migrations?

- Will Europe manage to reinvent itself and regenerate its economic and social dynamism?

- How many people with a "world-centric" perspective are needed to ensure we make thriveable decisions for our planet at all levels- global, national, regional and local?

- What will the fate of the poorest and least developed nations be? Will the SDG's be enough to help them lift our of the poverty trap in sustainable ways?

- Will the leap-frogging of exponential technologies to the developing world ensure a thriveable future for them?

While the sheer diversity and native talent of our species give us great hope for synergistic-innovations that will decode the Anthropocene Enigma, we are going to need all our wits, resources and connectivity to ensure that Era 4 does not end abruptly in a century or two. In the next section we are going to explore how we can "get our act together" within the framework of six synergistic-innovation pathways to ensure a thriveable future for us all.

These six innovation pathways each emerge from a dominant capital that needs to be regenerated in order to ensure our survival and thriving. The BioPsychoSocioTechno approach helps us think through the cross-impacts and synergies that emerge between the six pathways and the eight capitals, so that we can test our projects, organisations, innovations and designs for their ability to regenerate key capitals.

As billions more people gain access to vital resources, and build the trusted relationships needed for thriveable collaboration and transformation, proven global solutions abstracted into blueprints for thriveable outcomes can be shared amongst those whose awareness has risen to become conscious of the challenges and opportunities of our emerging global civilisation.

PART 8: SIX PATHWAYS TO A THRIVING FUTURE

36. Overview of the Six Pathways

If you wish to be a part of a thriving future that regenerates our biosphere and our global civilisation to be a more peaceful, sustainable and enjoyable place to live, then the best place to begin your journey is to assess your current thinking and practices using the six pathways to a thriving future. These pathways are:

1. Values and Visions- what do you imagine when look into the future where you currently are? What are your dreams, aspirations and priorities? What does a good life, community and society look like to you? How can you shift yourself and others toward a thriving ethical culture where you are? Do you know what your core values are, and how they might be changing?

2. Human Development- do you and people where you are have access to good healthcare and education? Are your and their basic needs being met? How much attention is being paid where you are to wellbeing and life-long learning?

3. Thriveable Economies- are there opportunities for good work and jobs where you are? Do those in charge govern fairly and honestly? How thriveable is the future of the economy where you are?

4. A Flourishing Biosphere- do you and those around you have access to healthy food and recreation in nature? Are there flourishing farms, forests and fisheries near you? Would you say that the natural world is being well treated and regenerated where you are, or are essential items such as water, sanitation, and enjoyable natural habitats scarce?

5. Resilient Habitats- are there good homes and healthy towns and cities where you live and work? Are the energy, power and building industries fossil-fuel based or renewable?

6. Circular Manufacturing and Mobility- are the goods and services where you are made and distributed in sustainable ways, or are they wasteful? How much recycling happens where you are? Are scarce resources, appliances and transport shared, or does everyone have to have their own?

The six pathways to a thriveable 2050 are related to each other in a causal sequence that generates the synergies we need for breakthrough innovations. Being able to harness the human energies and flows of ideas, aspirations and capabilities generated in Pathways One (*Values and Visions- Social Capital*) and Two (*Human Development- Human Capital*) in thriveable ways, requires the next generation of governance, economics and finance platforms in Pathway Three (*Thriveable Economies- Financial Capital*) to be able to embed True Future Value into the emerging global system.

Connecting up pockets of the future in the present through the coalesced authority, power and influence of the innovators and visionaries emerging in our organisations and institutions enables rapid scaling and embedding of the most appropriate solutions wherever they "pop" into existence. This then provides the muscle and intelligence required to empower and accelerate the regeneration of our natural, infrastructure and manufactured capitals so as to create thriveable habitats for all the world's people by 2050 through Pathways Four (*A Flourishing Biosphere- Natural Capital*), Five (*Resilient Habitats- Infrastructure Capital*) and Six

(*Circular Manufacturing and Mobility- Manufactured Capital*).

We need to redefine and redesign what the good life means to ensure we can all meet our basic needs and have the opportunity to reach toward a thriving future. The six pathways act as guide for our journey into the future, and also as a measuring stick for how much progress we are making.

37. Values and Visions- Setting Priorities

Today global flows of people, goods, services, finance, social networks, and hyper-connective technologies are interweaving markets, media, banks, hospitals, businesses, schools, universities, communities, and individuals more tightly together than ever. The resulting flows of information, knowledge and relationships are making our world not only hyperconnected but also more interdependent than ever before.

Our values pretty much determine our priorities, and also shape the nature of our visions, dreams and the possibilities we believe are open to us. Some people believe that their values are what they say or think they are, as in statements of belief. For example, "I have liberal values" or "I have conservative values" or "I have Christian values" or "I have Buddhist values".

Yet these are at best superficial, only slightly more consequential than our opinions and attitudes, which like the weather, are changeable. They are the result of our upbringing and our social conditioning, what our families and friends value and believe is important. This is only natural, and nothing to be ashamed of, but be aware that such values have proven to be very malleable. This is what the persuasion industries rely on to shift you to see the world from their point of view.

Our real values, however, are hidden deep in our unconscious, shaped in turn by generations of ancestors and life conditions that make you who you are right now. These deeper values change only slowly over time, as we grow and mature. Nearly 400 different psychological schools agree that there are eight or so developmental levels that people can go through in a lifetime, depending upon their own life path and circumstances. Every stage of development opens up new horizons, and brings to bear a different set of values, based on a perception of longer time horizons and a shift from egocentric to ethnocentric to worldcentric ways of being and thinking.

Until you become aware of what these deeper values are at some point in your life, you are acting out of a script written a long time ago, some of it by people you know and much by people you have never met. Most of us never question our deepest assumptions because we only discover what they are when life hits us over the head and forces us to re-examine them.

If our values make it our priority to build healthy communities and societies, then we will need to understand the key capital that develops them- social capital. According to the World Bank, social capital is not only an essential pillar of the economy. It also has a direct and irreplaceable monetary value. It accounts for more than 20% of the value of all goods and services produced (with peaks of 28% in the OECD countries), making it the most valuable 'industry' any country can boast. The trust embedded in the handshake is the founding institution of the market and society.

In order to grow social capital, we need to invest in the basics that create a civilized society. For working societies to endure, grow, and cohere, they need basic things that people believe *everyone should have*. In the UK, those things—those moral universals—are healthcare and media and welfare. In Germany, they are healthcare and media and welfare and higher education. And so on. Unfortunately in the USA it is these basic necessities that are being run down, leading to a rapid erosion of social capital.

The next few decades or so before 2050 will certainly be forcing most people on our planet to re-examine their values quite forcefully. And very few of them are ready for that. Are you?

38. Human Development

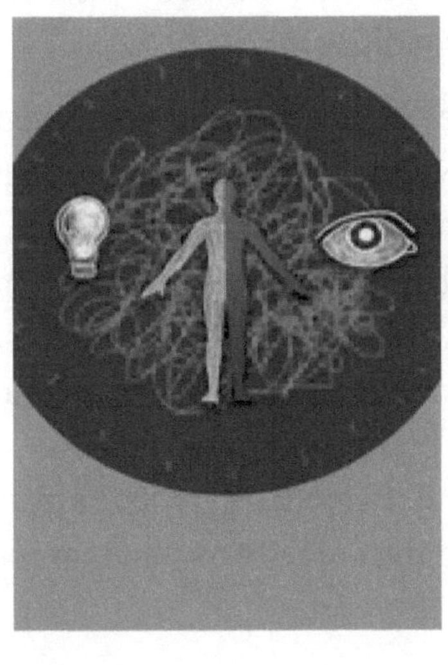

Good healthcare, education, media and welfare are key to wellbeing and life-long learning. In societies where the basic needs of all are met, it is possible for everyone, both rich and poor, to live fulfilling lives. Developing human capital is a top priority for civilized societies and organisations.

There is currently some form of compulsory education in almost all the countries on our planet. In the next 30 years more people will receive formal education than in all of human history. For example, the percentage of the global population without any schooling decreased from 36% in 1960 to 25% in 2000.

Education is rapidly moving beyond schooling and formal education alone to include non-formal and informal modes of instruction and learning, including traditional learning acquired in the home and community. Solving complex problems, systems thinking, working well in multi-disciplinary multi-cultural teams, thinking creatively and imaginatively- these are just a few of the key attributes needed to get ahead in the 21st century world of work and life. Yet they are not generally found in traditional curricula. Life-long learning is now a reality as the pace of change accelerates and skills become obsolete faster. Being an engaged and informed citizen as well as a contributor to the work and life of a community become key for thriving individuals, businesses and communities.

Artificial intelligence, assistive technologies, web-based delivery and interaction, cultivating meta-cognition and whole-bodied learning at home, on-the-job and in leisure and public spaces- we are just at the beginning of a revolution in how we learn, grow and develop as people, families, communities, organisations, nations and globally. We see the beginnings of not just a global brain emerging, but also a global heart with compassion, and a global "gut" that offers intuitive insights and nudges, and the courage to stand up for what is right and thriveable.

Human vision, imagination, development and learning are the core drivers of the shifts between the Stone Age, the Agricultural Age, the Industrial Age and now the information/Knowledge Age and what comes next. Without vision and imagination, we would not be able to see possibilities or invent the new and play creatively with it. Without learning and development, synergistic innovations based on those new ideas would not be possible, and we would still be large hairy apes walking upright in the savannah- or not here at all, given the hazardous life-conditions we have had to adapt to over the course of the past few hundred thousand years.

What it means to be human has changed several times during our evolution, and it is about to change again, as we deal with the massive accelerations in technology, our environment, politics, governance, economics and business and the way in which we learn and make decisions.

We can and should be strive to meet the basic needs of all by 2050, including the Sustainable Development Goals, which lay out 17 areas for a world that works for all of us by 2030. Climate action that keeps global warming to less than 2 degrees, and the regeneration of life below water and on land so that we live within our environmental ceilings, is a precondition for all else. In turn social goals that underpin the social floors for all of us include the elimination of poverty and hunger plus sanitation, clean water, healthcare and education made available to all.

39. Thriveable Economies

Pathway Three outlines what a regenerative, inclusive socioeconomic system looks like, and how we can get from here to there; how the true costs of our political economies can be reflected in true prices, encouraged by true taxation that encourages us to work, earn income and regenerate vital capitals while penalising activities that harm our stocks of natural, human and social capitals.

Each of us needs to find meaning and satisfaction in our life and work. The explosion of technologies and infrastructures brought about by the industrial and information ages now means most of us still manage to make a living, but are disconnected from our work and workplace. Unemployment in many countries is also very high, and workers have seen their wages drop quite dramatically over the past four decades relative to the rise in wealth of the richest 10%. The gap between the rich, middle classes and poor has continued to grow dramatically in the past 40 years. In developed countries the middle class in particular has seen its income flatten and fall during this period, while the richest 1% have seen dramatic gains from globalisation.

American Senator Elizabeth Warren put it well when she explained to an audience why governments and public services are vital to develop ourselves and our economies: "There is nobody in this country who got rich on their own. Nobody. You built a factory out there – good for you. But I want to be clear. You moved your goods to market on roads the rest of us paid for. You hired workers the rest of us paid to educate. You were safe in your factory because of police forces and fire forces that the rest of us paid for. You didn't have to worry that marauding bands would come and seize everything at your factory … Now look. You built a factory and it turned into something terrific or a great idea – God bless! Keep a hunk of it. But part of the underlying social contract is you take a hunk of that and pay forward for the next kid who comes along."

In some countries the social contract has been reduced to: "If you educate and train yourself diligently at great personal expense, you might be lucky to get a good job for a while. Because you are just a number in the statistics, as soon as you become obsolete you will have to retrain yourself at further great personal expense. Then you might be lucky to get a good job for another while. Make sure you save for your retirement, because by then there will be no one else to look after you. And healthcare- you're on your own".

How can we reinvent the social contract so that a thriveable economy becomes possible for all of us as a guaranteed outcome? What kind of a political economy will become possible in the next few decades, given the challenges we face in the exit turbulence of our current dysfunctional growth-at-all-costs policies? What does a regenerative, inclusive socioeconomic system look like, and how do we get from here to there?

As a starting point, the cost of carbon, water and other ecosystem services needs to be included in every economic activity, so that we can measure true, value, true costs and true profits. The ThriveAbility Equation that measures True Future Value creation, takes us to another level in this quest. Measuring True Future Value helps us make better decisions, compared with pure profit, economic value added, and shareholder value added measures.

40. A Flourishing Biosphere

Natural capital, or "nature", as we used to innocently call it, is the single most vital capital on our planet. If we do not regenerate our stocks of natural capital, everything we love and cherish starts dying around us.

Right now, every single one of the trillions of cells in your body is regenerating itself. Damage caused by free oxygen radicals, pollutants, and the natural breakdown of cells as they age, is continually being repaired, 24x7. New cells are being created to replace those dying cells, so that even though you may add a few grey hairs or wrinkles every year as you age, you can still function normally, and hopefully, thrive.

As health-conscious human beings, we worry justifiably about our weight, blood pressure, heart rate, cholesterol levels and so on, as we know there is a strong relationship between those indicators and our health. In the same way, our planetary biosphere has *nine indicators* which tell us if she is healthy or not, and right now she has a rising fever compounded by kidney and liver damage along with some lung damage caused by all the pollutants we are pumping into her air, water and oceans.

Just as you can be guaranteed a swift death if you smoke 100 cigarettes and drink a couple of bottles of spirits a day, so too can we guarantee the death of 90% of life on earth if we continue our current lifestyles and business as usual. We have already overshot four of the nine planetary boundaries that keep us and the rest of the biosphere alive:

- **climate change** caused by human emissions of greenhouse gases, mainly carbon dioxide, from the burning of fossil fuels in the past three centuries, so that we now have 400+ parts per million of CO2 in the atmosphere overheating our planet instead of 250 ppm a century or so ago (increasing risk zone);
- **biosphere integrity** where the sixth mass extinction of species has already reached a speed never before seen in the history of our planet both on land in in our oceans (high risk zone);
- **biogeochemical flows** where both phosphorous and nitrogen emissions are in the red, causing dead zones in waterways and coastal zones around the world (high risk zone);
- **land system change** involving the conversion of forests, grasslands, wetlands and other vegetation types to agricultural land plays a major role in biodiversity reduction, and has impacts on water flows and on the biogeochemical cycling of carbon, nitrogen and phosphorus and other important elements.

The good news is that the pendulum is swinging back toward regeneration as hundreds of millions of people around the planet engage in innovative ways of restoring natural habitats of all descriptions. Rainforest regeneration projects are beginning to have a positive impact in the Amazon and Southeast Asia, while conservation measures in Africa are beginning to slow the rate of deforestation there. Coral reef regeneration projects are underway and making progress in many parts of the world's oceans, with new species of coral being bred to deal with warmer oceans.

In our cities where vertical farming is taking hold, crops can be grown year-round under optimal conditions. One acre of skyscraper floor produces the equivalent of 10 to 20 traditional soil-based acres. Employing clean-room technologies means no pesticides or herbicides, so there's no agricultural runoff. Patterned after natural forest ecosystems, food forests (also known as "forest gardens") are designed permaculture systems that consist of a multi-layered edible "forest." Such a "forest" is composed almost entirely of perennial food plants, including a canopy of tall and dwarf fruit and nut trees, a fruit shrub layer, layers of perennial herbs, mushrooms and vegetables at the ground level, climbing plants, and root vegetables underground.

Several different approaches to reducing plastics pollution are being trialled, from the local to the global. There are two main challenges- cleaning up the plastics that are already in our rivers, lakes and oceans, and stopping those plastics from getting into the water in the first place. The ultimate solution is to reduce, reuse, recycle, of course, but that will take time to become common practice around our planet.

Aquaculture, the farming of seafood, is another area offering high hopes for feeding the world. There is evidence that the Chinese were farming fish in 5th century BCE, and the

Egyptians and Romans were great oyster cultivators as well, so aquaculture is not exactly new. What is new, however, is that since the 1980s, when growth rates allowing an economic return were achieved, world aquaculture production has increased from 7% of global fisheries to over 40%[v]. By 2024 the OECD estimates that aquaculture will produce more seafood than is caught in the world's oceans.

The productivity of aquaculture has also risen dramatically: it takes between 1.5 to 3 kg of feed to produce one kg of chicken or pork, while 1kg of feed produces 1kg of rainbow trout. While salmon, tuna, prawns, oysters, abalone and other high-end seafood are some of the most popular products of aquaculture today, tilapia, molluscs, carp, catfish and crustaceans are expected to grow dramatically by 2030.

At any given time, close to half the population of the developing world is suffering from waterborne diseases associated with inadequate provision of water and sanitation services. There are about four billion cases of diarrheal disease per year, resulting in about one or two million deaths, some ninety percent of which, tragically, are in children under the age of five.

Cholera, typhoid fever and hepatitis A are caused by bacteria, and are among the most common diarrheal diseases. Other illnesses, such as dysentery, are caused by parasites that live in water contaminated by the faeces of sick individuals. Lakes and streams which people use for drinking water, bathing and defecating are sources of disease, as is water left by natural disasters. Tsunamis, hurricanes and floods leave victims in ankle-deep water, amid destroyed sewage pipes.

A number of social entrepreneurs have teamed up with different partners worldwide to address the interlinked problems of water, electricity and sanitation. Innovative ways of filtering water to provide clean drinking water without killer bacteria and viruses in them. For example, the "EKOCENTER" is a modular community market that is run by a local woman entrepreneur and also provides safe water, solar power, Internet access, and more. It operates "off-the-grid," from a kiosk that becomes a hub of community activity by providing a place of commerce as well as safe drinking water, solar power and wireless communication.

Other functionality that can be added to jump-start community development includes social facilities and entertainment; power generation for charging phones; cooling/refrigeration of vaccines; education opportunities; and much more. There are now over 100 EKOCENTERs in Kenya, Tanzania, Rwanda, Ethiopia, Ghana and Vietnam and Southern Africa, and they continue to expand globally.

These are just a few of the inspiring examples of innovative projects that give us hope that we can reverse the damage we have done to the world's ecosystems in time.

41. Resilient Habitats

In order to conserve and regenerate the vitality of the earth's key ecosystems, we are going to have to transition our energy and power industries from fossil fuels to renewables globally within the next few decades. Smarter buildings with wiser users and a zero net-energy standard for all new buildings must become the norm, together with a massive retro-fitting program of existing buildings to make them much more energy-efficient.

Sustainable Development Goal 11 aims to make cities and human settlements inclusive, safe, resilient and sustainable. By 2030, it is projected that 6 out of 10 people will be urban dwellers. Despite numerous planning challenges, well-managed cities and other human settlements can be incubators for innovation and ingenuity and key drivers of sustainable development.

However, as more people migrate to cities in search of a better life and urban populations grow, housing issues intensify. Already in 2014, 30 per cent of the urban population lived in slum-like conditions; in sub-Saharan Africa, the proportion was 55 per cent, the highest of any region. Globally, more than 880 million people were living in slums in 2014. This estimate does not include people in inadequate or unaffordable housing (defined as costing more than 30 per cent of total monthly household income).

Managing solid waste is also problematic in densely populated areas. In many developing regions, less than half of solid waste is safely disposed of. As per capita waste generation continues to rise, the collection and safe disposal of solid waste will continue to require serious attention. Urban air pollution also challenged cities around the world, causing illness and millions of premature deaths annually. Around half the global urban population is exposed to air pollution levels at least 2.5 times higher than maximum standards set by the World Health Organization.

The quest for sustainable and coordinated urban development starts with national policies and regional development plans. As of 2015, 142 countries had a national urban policy in place or under development. Those countries are home to 75 per cent of the world's urban population.

Worldwide, about 1.2 billion people have no access to electricity and the development benefits it brings, and 1 billion more have access only to unreliable electricity networks. Nearly 3 billion people rely on traditional biomass (such as wood and charcoal) for cooking and heating.

Energy is the golden thread that connects economic growth, social equity, and environmental sustainability. This lack of modern energy services stifles income-generating activities and hampers the provision of basic services such as health care and education. In addition, smoke from polluting and inefficient cooking, lighting, and heating devices kills an estimated four million people a year and causes a range of chronic illnesses and other negative health impacts. These emissions are also important drivers of climate change and local environmental degradation.

The global economy will require big investments in infrastructure as populations and the middle class grow — especially in energy systems and cities. The demand for new infrastructure could top $90 trillion over 2015-2030, according to The New Climate Economy's 2014 report, Better Growth, Better Climate. The drive to cut carbon emissions changes the mix of this spending. Clean energy, efficient power grids and energy-efficient buildings are on the menu. The energy and transport sectors make up two-thirds of the needs, a 2016 McKinsey report estimates. Water and waste take up a fifth. See the chart below. Most of the spending is needed in emerging markets.

Investments in renewable energy and electricity systems in the developing world are now outpacing that of the developed world. As the price of solar, wind and biofuels continues to drop and offer savings on existing energy sources, these investments are effectively a "no-brainer" for these countries. Picture a new home, covered in solar tiles that generate enough electricity to power both the house and the car. The Tesla Powerwall - a rechargeable lithium ion battery weighing roughly 200 pounds that can be easily mounted on any wall, solves the problem of obtaining power when the sun goes down.

The Tesla Gigafactory's planned annual battery production capacity of 35 gigawatt-hours (GWh) will help accelerate the world's transition to sustainable energy, as electric vehicles need to be produced in sufficient volume to force change in the automobile industry. With a planned production rate of 500,000 cars per year by 2020, Tesla alone will require today's entire worldwide production of lithium ion batteries.

In order to "Decarbonise the Power Sector", we need not only renewable energy sources such as solar, wind, biofuels, geo-thermal, hydro-electricity and non-polluting nuclear, but also a "smart grid" which can distribute and use the available electricity as economically and intelligently as possible. Smart grids are Era 4 electric power grids that enhance the efficiency and reliability of the infrastructure required to power modern buildings and civilisations. They integrate automated controls, high-power converters, Internet based communications systems, sensing and metering technologies, and sophisticated energy management techniques that optimise the whole grid.

Smart grids and intelligent buildings will be a powerful force for good in helping us keep global warming below 2 degrees and also save money on energy bills for everyone, while keeping us well lit, at the right temperature and able to cook, clean, play and entertain ourselves in thriveable habitats. Looking into the future, a smart home will be like a human central nervous system, with a central platform, or "brain" at the core. Individual homebots will radiate out from this platform and perform a wide variety of tasks, including supervising other bots. Homebots can be as diverse as their roles: big, small, invisible (such as the software that runs systems or products), shared, and personal. Some homebots will be companions or assistants, others wealth planners and accountants. We will have homebots as coaches, window washers, and household managers, throughout our home.

In the near future expect to see more items in our living space become interconnected—the formative first stage of a new home ecosystem. In five years, numerous tools and devices in the home will be affected. And in a few decades in developed parts of the world, smart homes will become commonplace and will regularly feature devices and systems with independent intelligence and apparent emotion.

In the developing world in transition into the modern era, or leapfrogging directly to the thriveable economy, we will find the emergence of local, bottom up smart grids. Here we will find distributed renewable energy and communications systems such as the Ekocentre connect up with other local forms of infrastructure to facilitate community and agricultural planning, energy and resource sharing as well as educational and entertainment functions. Smarter communities and regions will link up to form more thriveable habitats for all their inhabitants, as well as connecting to smart cities and the smart grids required to facilitate their activities.

42. Circular Manufacturing & Mobility

Thriveable habitats are composites of regenerative infrastructures and manufactured capital integrated with natural capital in ways that are conducive to human thriving and the wellbeing of key native species in local ecosystems.

A thriveable habitat provides the foundation for the development and regeneration of human, relationship, social and intellectual capitals. The flows and exchanges of people, goods, money and information are facilitated in thriveable habitats by regenerative and inclusive mobility systems that support closed loop, circular economy approaches and sharing economy principles.

Most of our infrastructure capital and its intelligence in Pathway Five is hidden behind the surfaces of the roads, bridges, stations, airports, hospitals, shopping malls, schools, factories, power stations, offices and homes we take for granted every day. Infrastructure acts like our basic organ systems and skeleton that make it possible for our senses and limbs to engage with the world, which in turn make Pathway Six possible.

Pathway Six and manufactured capital is akin to our skin, acting as the interface between us, others, the environment and the stuff and systems we interact with. We see, feel, hear, smell and taste everything we interact with in Pathway Six – from the interiors of our homes, cars, public transport, to the interiors of our offices, factories and other places of work, to our computing and communications devices, to the clothing and accessories we wear and the people we meet and live/work/play with. A place of sensory delights, as well as unwanted substances, smells and sounds.

This is the world of designer and "women's magazines", interior decoration, the physical underpinning of the world of culture and the arts, our paintings, sculptures, musical instruments and all the toys and games we have or ever will play with. And when we travel we experience the vast investments in manufactured capitals superimposed on the backbone of infrastructures, from swanky airport and aircraft interiors to the more functional interiors of trains, stations, buses and taxis, and the insides of hotels and restaurants and resorts and…..

In fact, in modernist, materialist societies, large numbers of people create their entire identity out of this world of manufactured capital, from the clothes they wear to the car they drive to the restaurants they enjoy and the clubs and concerts they attend to the devices in their pockets.

Consumerist capitalism was in fact designed to make this world of effervescent novelty and rapid obsolescence the only game in town for the suburban and urban middle classes and elites. It is still today the dominant game being played globally by the rising classes and those in power. And that, right there, is one of our greatest challenges – how can we develop creative, more thriveable lifestyles that do not involve such conspicuous and wasteful consumption? There are currently several paths that have begun to deepen within Pathway Six, including:

The Circular Economy – what began as the "cradle-to-cradle" movement and "biomimicry" is coalescing into an approach to design which demands that we reduce, reuse, recycle and upcycle all materials through regenerative design approaches. The circular economy movement began with The Ellen MacArthur Foundation in 2010. Its aim is to accelerate the transition to the circular economy. Since its creation the charity has emerged as a global thought leader, establishing the circular economy on the agenda of decision makers across business, government and academia. The Foundation's work focuses on education, business innovation, economic reports, systemic initiatives and communications.

Redefining the Good Life – various movements against conspicuous, materialist, consumerist ways of living are also coalescing into a broad spectrum of alternative lifestyle and mainstream lifestyle choices. I believe it is important for us to each begin to tell our own stories about how we are personally engaging with each of the six pathways toward a more thriveable world and a better, richer, deeper and more meaningful life for ourselves and those we care about. My hope is that the models and frameworks used in this book will help you to do that in your own life, and share that with others;

Sharing Economy – whether it be accommodation, ride-sharing, car-sharing, tool sharing or any other form of sharing, the sharing economy has become a major trend in the past decade. A recent study by PricewaterhouseCoopers[vi], looked at five components of the sharing economy: travel, car sharing, finance, staffing and streaming. It found that global spending in these sectors totalled about $15 billion, or only about 5% of the total spending in those areas. The report also forecasts a possible increase of "sharing economy" spending in these areas to $335 billion by 2025, which would be about 50% of the total spending in these areas. As peer-to-peer commercial exchange blurs the lines between the personal and the professional, how will the economy, government regulation, what it means to have a job, and our social fabric be affected?

Thriveable Habitat Design – new ways of designing human habitats are also gaining traction, applying integral, systemic approaches to both urban and rural habitats that integrate wellbeing/healthcare, transport/mobility, sustainable business, natural resilience and research and education in the design approach. Design and innovation are both crucial to creating thriveable and desirable futures, yet if they occur in contexts that are too narrow (or "siloed" i.e. in narrow silos of activity or disciplines), they run the risk of being difficult or impossible to implement in the face of highly complex, inter-connected challenges, also know as "wicked problems". Most of the big problems we face as a species are now wicked, given the success we have had in solving the simple and complicated problems.

So the really difficult challenge is: how can we transcend siloes and encourage systemic thinking and actions across habitats at different scales, so that we have a chance of arriving at a desirable, thriveable future for all stakeholders?

Like the layers on Google Earth maps, the scales and boundaries of habitats can be watersheds, ecosystems, biomes, islands, continents, or human defined boundaries such as a single home, to a small community or town, to a city, to a region, a nation state or an entire planet. Clearly though, the design process relies on human stakeholders to make it work, which is why one normally begins with the politically defined boundaries before moving onto the natural systems boundaries. Within these boundaries at different levels of scale, we find that our current systems of governance split responsibility for different social functions into different departments and various kinds of entities suited to the purpose of each function.

Being able to think, act and regulate systemically across existing siloes is one of the most difficult yet critical things we need to do well, which is why developing the next generation of integrated leaders is so vital to creating a thriving future for us all on earth.

PART 9: IMAGINE

43. An Invitation to Your Pragmatic Imagination

We can use our imaginations for sense-making about what already exists and how it works, or sense-breaking, where we need to come up with highly imaginative ideas that have never been tried before. Innovators are generally sense-breakers, making what previously seemed impossible, possible.

Sense-making and logical reasoning is a highly valued skill in our modern economy. In fact, we have elevated this skill to the very top of what we define as excellence and achievement in education and most careers. There are two types of logic- deductive and inductive.

Deductive reasoning starts out with a general statement, or hypothesis, and examines the possibilities to reach a specific, logical conclusion. For example, the scientific method uses deduction to test hypotheses and theories. Deductive reasoning usually follows "top-down" steps. First, there is a premise, then a second premise, and finally an inference.

Inductive reasoning is the opposite of deductive reasoning. Inductive reasoning makes broad generalizations from specific observations. Basically, there is data, then conclusions are drawn from the data. In inductive inference, we go from the specific to the general, or "bottom-up". We make many observations, discern a pattern, make a generalization, and infer an explanation or a theory.

When things get very complex and uncertain, however, we need a third type of reasoning, which is much less taught and used- abductive reasoning. Abductive reasoning usually starts with an incomplete set of observations and proceeds to the likeliest possible explanation for the group of observations. It often entails making an educated guess after observing a phenomenon for which there is no clear explanation. It requires a Sherlock Homes type of intuition and pattern recognition, which is generally more "right-brained" than "left-brained".

Abductive reasoning shifts us from using the imagination for sense-making to sense-breaking. Imagination for sense-breaking and breakthrough innovations also has to be pragmatic- in other words, it has to not only understand the known, current situation, but it also has to widen the gap between the known and unfamiliar to pro-actively imagine the actual in light of meaningful, purposeful possibilities.

The generative side of the innovation spectrum is especially critical in a world that requires radically new visions and actions. Instead of only analysing things, the pragmatic imagination synthesises new combinations that have never been tried before, in order to invent the truly new.

Because the imagination is not under conscious control, we need to understand, find, and design ways to set it in motion and scaffold it for play and purpose, encouraging speculation, experimentation and free play. It is especially important that we create safe spaces for such purposeful experimentation and creative play, allowing participants to harness their visual and emotional faculties in creative ways to reach outcomes that could not have been imagined before.

Research and experience demonstrate that worldviews transform through communal exchange, and thereby evolve not through survival of the fittest, but transformation of all. We are co-evolving with each other, our infrastructure and our technology, mediated by webs of cultural significance and hierarchies of power, authority and influence. It has been scientifically proven that engaging your imagination with desirable outcomes rewires your brain. What you have in your hands is a playground for your imagination, to learn about and play with all the exciting new possibilities that are capable of generating a thriving world in our lifetimes.

44. The Shape of a Regenerative, Distributive Economy

Imagine a world powered by renewable energy, where all human beings thrive in resilient habitats; where businesses operate in a circular economy that regenerates natural capital, without a particle of waste, and are led by enlightened leaders whose goal is to maximize the thriving of all their stakeholders; where each individual is empowered to pursue their passion and make a living in service to others; where governance systems are transparent, effective and wise in the ways in which they deliver their services to their communities and populations; and where intercultural appreciation and insight enriches the exchanges between the diverse worldviews and cultures embraced by humankind.

Does that sound like an impossible dream, or pie in the sky? Every single one of these "pockets of the future" is currently observable in the present, right here and right now, somewhere in the world. It is just that the future is distributed unevenly, and sometimes hard to see when one is up to one's neck in alligators and trying to drain the swamp.

The cornerstone capital on which the health of our world depends is social capital. This is why it forms the bedrock of Pathway One, Values and Visions. If we cannot trust each other, our corporations, governments and "leaders" to do the right thing, then our civilisation, such as it is, will fail. To synergise social capital, we need to appreciate how it is formed through a mixture of all the other capitals that it is made up of: human, relationship, intellectual, infrastructure, manufactured, natural and financial. And also appreciate how this melange creates different kinds of value for different kinds of people.

To make good happen we must design our organisations, products, networks and social institutions as autocatalytic, self-sustaining interactions between the eight capitals, in regenerative, distributive ways. We can use the six pathways to 2050 as a map to help position where we are and the next steps we must take on our respective journeys toward good.

That might sound overly complicated, but on a day to day basis, we are already intuitively equipped to do exactly that- we know how important our relationships with our friends, family and colleagues are; we also know that our reputation and that of those we associate with is key for our continued success personally and professionally; and we are also well aware that we can use money, technology, infrastructure and knowledge to make our lives work better.

And whatever your political persuasion, there is also a common sense acknowledgement that if the rich get so rich that everyone else despises them, there will be social unrest; we also know as common sense that burning up the resources of our planet faster than we can regenerate them will leave a scorched earth for future generations; and we also know deep down that a fairer world will be a happier world, where there is at least equality of opportunity- a world where the social resources for healthcare, education, transport and the key infrastructure needed to underpin all of that are available to all, and not just a select few.

Many societies today are already well along the journey to being genuinely regenerative and distributive- Costa Rica, Denmark, Sweden, Norway and Finland for example. Even Bhutan. Of course, every society will need to take this journey in its own way that reflects its culture, history and other unique characteristics, and some will find it much harder than others given their dependence on fossil fuels, mass consumerism and financial elites who often block the moves needed to go from making bad things happen, to making good things happen.

45. Thriveable Transformation

In 1974 Psychologist Prof. Clare Graves summarized his three decades of research into adult development as follows:

"What I am proposing is that the psychology of the mature human being is an unfolding, emergent, oscillating, spiraling process marked by progressive subordination of older, lower-order behavior systems to newer, higher-order systems as man's existential problems change. These systems alternate between focus upon the external world, and attempts to change it, and focus upon the inner world, and attempts to come to peace with it, with the means to each end changing in each alternately prognostic system." Thriveable Transformation integrates these developmental insights with integral psychology, big history, evolutionary science and cognitive science, to provide an accelerated process for transformation at individual, team, organizational, community and regional scales. Let's call these "entities".

The Seven Steps of Thriveable Transformation follow an alternating sequence of "outside-in" and "inside-out" logic. Step 1 begins with an outside-in understanding of the context of the entity in focus. For an individual, for example, the context might include family, a team or a community. Step 2 then flips into an inside-out mode of inquiry, asking what it is that is motivating the entity in question, what is the stance of that entity, how does it feel about things, what are its values and priorities that shape its needs? This logic continues throughout the seven steps, until the final integration of all of these inquiries in Step 7, which is also offers us the opportunity to experience a transformational moment or two.

Graves' research and subsequent work by a host of others in the four decades since, have confirmed his early suspicions that human society is facing a period of fundamental change, "the most difficult, but at the same time the most exciting transition the human race has faced to date." Graves believed that humanity was at the beginning of "not merely a transition to a new level of existence, but the start of a new movement in the symphony of human history". Graves called the first six developmental stages of adults "first-tier", and the momentous leap occurs in the transition into the seventh and eight stages of development, which he called "second-tier".

Thriveability is designed using a second-tier template that includes two "upstretch packages"- the first for peak to exiting achievers and the second for peak to exiting individualists. The key principle is that "Thriveability starts with me and is everyone's responsibility"- this works with a ladder and a set of evolving views from each rung of the ladder, so that decision makers and investors at all levels from families to communities to cities to organizations to countries to global bodies can make more Thriveable decisions. The Thriveability Template recognises that each level of development is an interconnected ecosystem of players with complementary strengths who ideally need to co-evolve Thriveability in their parts of the ecosystem, helping unblock blockages motivated by propositions which are irresistible to each rung on the ladder.

Real 2nd tier applies acupuncture to dysfunctional parts of the first-tier memetic system, requiring it to know and be an expression of the healthy versions of all six levels. If the "2nd Tier" claimant is seriously dysfunctional or lacking themselves in any of the first-tier systems, that will tarnish the intervention. It is not so much just another stage, as that strategic psychological helicopter hovering over the entire first tier system of being and doing. Which is why the strategists in the FlexFlow 7th stage are so critical. Flexflow is a holistic acupuncturist, while the 8th stage, Globalview, is a planetary shaman

46. Seven Dimensions of Thriveable Transformation

There are seven dimensions to thriveable transformation, which follow the outside-in, inside-out dynamics that characterise developmental processes. The first six of these dimensions, or steps, start with the outside-in understanding of one's context, and end with the inside-out integration of one's own evolutionary self. Step 7 then builds on the learnings and insights from steps 1 to 6, dramatically expanding one's ability to generate transformative moments and design thriveable futures:

Step 1 - SEE - Understand Your Context – What is the structure of the system that operates as the context for the entity? What are the parts, what constitutes the whole? How do those parts inter-relate and affect each other? Is the context functional or dysfunctional? Why? How does the past influence the present and enable or constrain future possibilities in the context? What are the Bio, Psycho, Socio and Techno trends, threats and opportunities?

Step 2 - FEEL - Examine Your Values & Priorities – What motivates you as an entity in this situation? What are your/its aspirations and frustrations? What core values are enabling or constraining the possibilities in this situation, and how are they shaping the priorities of the entity? What is the current trajectory of the entity? Where is it heading if nothing is done or changed? Which relationships between the entity and significant others are working, which are dissonant?

Step 3 - ALIGN - Align with Enabling Trends & Forces – What are the main tensions between the entity and its context? How is its context changing? What are the "Givens" in this situation? What trends favor the instinctive direction the entity is moving in or desires to move toward? What deeper forces in the environment around the entity and the systemic structures it is part of, enable or constrain this movement? What are the strong attractors and repellants? How can the tensions between these trends, forces and the desires of the entity be aligned generatively?

Step 4 - MOTIVATE - Act from Stratified Insights – What is the center-of-gravity of the entity in terms of its values? How healthy and appropriate are those values for the entity and its key stakeholders? What value-systems are driving each key stakeholder? How resonant or dissonant are those values with the preferences of the entity itself? What are the "hot buttons" and |cold buttons" for each stakeholder? What is the readiness for change of the entity and its key stakeholders? Are they stuck/blocked, or flowing in a good direction?

Step 5 - MAP - Map Your Journey to Thriving – Which of the six pathways to thriving set out in the book "Making Good Happen- Pathways to a Thriving Future", is the entity aware of and engaged with? Map the key activities of the entity for each pathway, and those of its key stakeholders in its context. Dig deeper into the processes and relationships that maintain the status quo, and those that can lend themselves to change and transformation. Use a strategic influence map to identify key leverage points for emergence in the system. Where are the warm synergies?

Step 6 - INTEGRATE - Integrate Your Evolutionary Self – What is the emerging purpose of the entity that might enable it to change or transform within its context, or even shape its context? What is the unique contribution of the entity to the systems it forms a part of? What is its "genius"? How can the entity become more coherent by transcending and integrating itself and its current context?

We now move onto the master move in thriveable transformation- Step 7 - designing thriveable futures, where we bring together our developmental journey (stance and stages) with our social/emotional and cognitive bases from which our tools for transformation spring.

47. Designing Thriveable Futures

Step 7 - DESIGN - Designing Thriveable Futures relies on the art and science of generating transformative moments that shift entities and the warm systems they are in, into healthier, more thriveable states. The outcome of the sequence of the first six steps is a new stance which opens up new possibilities. Your "stance" is how you position yourself to what is different from and other than you. Your experience then follows your stance. This is well known from social-emotional theory which distinguishes "stages" of meaning making each of which defines a different stance toward oneself and others in the social world. Your stance may thus stand in the way of fully transformative thinking, and since stance is held unconsciously, transformative thought and action will remain impossible for you until you change your stance.

The world you see as "yours", is a result of the interaction between your stance and your "tools", which are both cognitive and psychological tools that make you more comfortable with contradiction and uncertainty that your stance may be poised to deny. A key to thriveable transformation is the insight that being attentive to what is emerging, you might have a chance to realize that your way of perceiving and thinking of something is limited, and less than thriveable. This realization could then have an impact on your stance, in the direction of becoming more highly aware of contradictions in what you encounter in the world. And this, in turn, could then lead you to having different experiences of, and in, the world. As a result, we can say there is a complete feedback loop between Stance, Tools, and Experiences.

The most powerful force for thriveable transformation in our challenging world today, is the ability to develop a new cognitive stance toward reality that directly contradicts what we take for granted, or swallow whole without reflection. If thinking for yourself still has meaning in the internet age, it amounts to including opposites and potentials in your thinking which open you up to new experiences and possibilities., informed by the sequence of what you have learned in the first six steps of thriveable transformation.

Teaching and learning integral, critical, complex and realistic thinking is the first step to realizing thriveable, transformative designs and moments in your own life and that of the others you engage with. In designing thriveable futures, you will need to reflect often on three questions to enhance your own success and ensure that of others through win-win-win dynamics:

•   **"What should I do, for whom?"**- reframe your identity and its sources (your work, family, possessions, religion and so on) to be more conducive to co-creating thriveable futures for yourself, your organisation and your world (your social-emotional base);

•   **"What can I do, what are my options?"**- How can you learn to engage with concepts and designs with a transformational complexity beyond your current capacity for transformative thought structures? (your cognitive base);

- **"How am I doing?"**- what feedback is the world giving you and your current way of being and operating? What are you perceiving, and what are you projecting?

Leaders in general must rethink their thinking to co-create thriveable outcomes through novel, emerging situations, especially in transforming social and business models. The north star for new social and business models must be thriveability for all stakeholders and all life on our planet. For culture transformations in organizations this means that corporate cultures open to transformational thinking have a much better chance of being transformational than organizations adhering to logical-thinking schemes which abound in departmental silos. This new integral vision requires lifelong and steady commitment to transformations of consciousness and constant revisioning of our models of self-and-other-seeing and -relating.

48. Healing Ourselves, Healing Our Planet

So, what will you do? How can you be part of the momentous leap, and make a difference that shifts not only mindsets, but also transforms cultures, social systems and the world around you?

This involves a two-step process- first, healing ourselves; then, step two involves applying that learning in some practical way that can be a part of the much bigger process of healing our planet.

There are generally four steps to healing ourselves-

- **Waking up-** becoming more aware and mindful of what is happening inside ourselves, and in the people and world around us; getting to grips with our strengths, weaknesses, and the opportunities and threats in our lives and careers;

- **Cleaning up-** all of us carry some baggage from the past, often referred to as our "shadow". There are many wonderful ways in which we can liberate the hidden energy in this shadow that is blocking us from taking the next steps we need to take to realise our dreams and ambitions;

- **Growing up-** we all have parts of ourselves that are still stuck in various immature stages of development, and which can get in the way of our journey through life. Again, working on developing ourselves and becoming a fully accountable adult in every area of our lives yields major benefits;

- **Showing up-** once we are fully accountable and responsible, we become dramatically more effective in using our capabilities to make a difference. We can see further, act faster, and go deeper in anything we set out to do, with less effort= and inspire others to do the same.

Remember that there are some 700 million other people at various stages in the momentous leap right now- you are not alone. And you can find them wherever you are, no matter what your interests, capabilities, passions and the current state of your networks and relationships. In order to close the momentous environmental and social gaps of our time, connecting up with like-minded others to align around things you care about and that really make a difference, is crucial.

The rewards of healing yourself, and healing our planet at the same time, are immense. The journey is well worth the effort. No matter where you are on your own journey, applying some of the thinking and frameworks in this book to improve your own practices and skills will help you become more focused and powerful in your efforts.

I have deliberately avoided annotating this book with endless footnotes and endnotes so as to focus on the main learning points, but there is a resources section at the end that can guide you to find additional information in whatever area you are interested in. From my own four decades of experience as a social and environmental activist, businessman and world traveller, as well as a more than two decades as an integral practitioner, I can assure you that you are in for the most exciting journey possible, the moment you take your first step.

Your fellow travellers are already out there, waiting for you to connect up with them. May the wind be at your back, and your companions resourceful as you undertake your journey together!

References & Sources

1. The Momentous Leap - Thriveable Transformation in the 21st Century. Dr Robin Lincoln Wood. 2018

2. Making Good Happen- Pathways to a Thriving Future. Dr Robin Lincoln Wood. 2017

3. Synergise! 21st Century Leadership. Dr Robin Lincoln Wood. 2017

4. A Leaders Guide to ThriveAbility. Dr Robin Lincoln Wood. 2015

5. The Trouble with Paradise: A Humorous Enquiry into the Puzzling Human Condition in the 21st Century. Dr Robin Lincoln Wood. 2014

6. LifeShift 2020 – A Companion Guide to the Great Shift. Dr Robin Lincoln Wood. 2009

7. The Great Shift: Catalysing the Second Renaissance. Dr Robin Lincoln Wood. 2009

8. Managing Complexity: How Businesses can Adapt and Prosper in the Connected Economy. Dr Robin Lincoln Wood. 2000

9. Spiral Dynamics- Mastering Values, Leadership and Change. Don Edward Beck and Christopher C. Cowan. Blackwell Publishing. 2005

10. A Theory of Everything- An Integral Vision for Business, Politics, Science and Spirituality. Ken Wilber. Shambhala Press. 2001.

11. The nine planetary boundaries of the Stockholm Resilience Institute (SRI)

Stratospheric ozone layer, Biodiversity, Chemicals dispersion, Climate Change, Ocean acidification, Freshwater consumption and the global hydrological cycle, Land system change, Nitrogen and phosphorus inputs to the biosphere and oceans, Atmospheric aerosol loading.

12. Global Footprint Network's footprint calculations (GFN)

Global Footprint Network is an international think tank working to advance sustainability through use of the Ecological Footprint, a resource accounting tool that measures how much nature we have, and how much we use. This tool is unique in making overshoot measurable – through detailed resource accounts for nations, cities and individuals.

13. World Resource Institute's Protocols for community scale

Global Protocol for Community-scale Greenhouse Gas Emissions (also called the "community protocol"). This landmark effort represents a significant step forward in harmonizing emissions measurement and reporting processes for cities of all sizes and geographies: the community protocol will be piloted in selected cities to establish a single minimum global standard for community-scale greenhouse gas (GHG) emissions measurement. A transparent, consistent and common approach provides cities with a much-needed tool for effective climate action planning and financing.

14.   GHG emissions (WRI)

Standard for community-scale greenhouse gas (GHG) emissions.

15.   World Business Council for Sustainable Development's Vision 2050

The WBCSD's cornerstone Vision 2050 report calls for a new agenda for business laying out a pathway to a world in which nine billion people can live well, and within the planet's resources, by mid-century. The report is a consensus piece that was compiled by 29 leading global companies from 14 industries and is the result of an 18 month long combined effort between CEOs and experts, and dialogues with more than 200 companies and external stakeholders in some 20 countries.

The report features a set of agreed must haves. They represent vital developments that the report's stakeholders hope organizations will consider putting in place within the next decade, to help ensure a steady course towards global sustainability is set. Ultimately, they are intended to provide a springboard for dialogue and debate.

16.   Action 2020 programs (WBCSD)

Created by the World Business Council for Sustainable Development (WBCSD) and its member companies, Action2020 is our platform for sustainability in action. It's the roadmap for how business can positively influence environmental and social trends while strengthening their own resilience to issues like climate change, demographic dynamics and skills shortages. Based on the latest scientific consensus, Action2020 sets an agenda for business to act on sustainable development to 2020 and beyond.

17.   SPI (Social Progress Index)

The 2014 Social Progress Index reveals striking differences across countries in their social performance, highlights the very different strengths and weaknesses of individual countries, and provides concrete guidance for national policy agendas.

The Index is the sum of three dimensions: Basic Human Needs, Foundations of Wellbeing, and Opportunity. Each dimension is made up of four equally weighted individual components scored on an objective scale from 0–100. This scale is determined by identifying the best and worst global performance on each indicator by any country in the last 10 years and using these to set the maximum (100) and minimum (0) bounds. Thus, Social Progress Index scores are realistic benchmarks rather than abstract measures. The scaling allows us to track absolute, not just relative, country performance.

18.   HPI (Happy Planet Index)

The HPI measures what matters: the extent to which countries deliver long, happy, sustainable lives for the people that live in them. The Index uses global data on life expectancy, experienced well-being and Ecological Footprint to calculate this.

The index is an efficiency measures, it ranks countries on how many long and happy lives they produce per unit of environmental input.

19.   GCI (Good Country Index)

It measures what each country on earth contributes to the common good of humanity, and what it takes away. Using a wide range of data from the U.N. and other international organisations, it is given each country a balance-sheet to show at a glance whether it's a net creditor to mankind, a burden on the planet, or something in between.

It's important to explain that we are not making any moral judgments about countries. What is meant by a Good Country is something much simpler: it's a country that contributes to the greater good.

20.   GRI (Global Reporting Initiative)

GRI has pioneered and developed a comprehensive Sustainability Reporting Framework that is widely used around the world. A sustainability report is a report published by a company or organization about the economic, environmental and social impacts caused by its everyday activities. A sustainability report also presents the organization's values and governance model and demonstrates the link between its strategy and its commitment to a sustainable global economy. GRI's mission is to make sustainability reporting standard practice for all companies and organizations. Its Framework is a reporting system that provides metrics and methods for measuring and reporting sustainability-related impacts and performance.

21.   UN Global Compact

The UN Global Compact is a strategic policy initiative for businesses that are committed to aligning their operations and strategies with ten universally accepted principles in the areas of human rights, labour, environment and anti-corruption. By doing so, business, as a primary driver of globalization, can help ensure that markets, commerce, technology and finance advance in ways that benefit economies and societies everywhere.

22.   Cradle-to-cradle (C2C)

Cradle to Cradle design (also referred to as Cradle to Cradle, C2C, cradle 2 cradle, or regenerative design) is a biomimetic approach to the design of products and systems. It models human industry on nature's processes viewing materials as nutrients circulating in healthy, safe metabolisms. It suggests that industry must protect and enrich ecosystems and nature's biological metabolism while also maintaining a safe, productive technical metabolism for the high-quality use and circulation of organic and technical nutrients. Put simply, it is a holistic economic, industrial and social framework that seeks to create systems that are not only efficient but also essentially waste free. The model in its broadest sense is not limited to industrial design and manufacturing; it can be applied to many aspects of human civilization such as urban environments, buildings, economics and social systems.

23.   Circular economy

The circular economy is a generic term for an industrial economy that is, by design or intention, restorative and in which material flows are of two types, biological nutrients, designed to re-enter the biosphere safely, and technical nutrients, which are designed to circulate at high quality without entering the biosphere.

24.   Millennium Ecosystem Assessment tool

The Millennium Ecosystem Assessment, released in 2005, is an international synthesis by over 1000 of the world's leading biological scientists that analyses the state of the Earth's ecosystems and provides summaries and guidelines for decision-makers. It concludes that human activity is having a significant and escalating impact on the biodiversity of world ecosystems, reducing both their resilience and bio capacity. The report refers to natural systems as humanity's "life-support system", providing essential "ecosystem services". The assessment measures 24 ecosystem services concluding that only four have shown improvement over the last 50 years, fifteen are in serious decline, and five are in a stable state overall, but under threat in some parts of the world.

25.   WEF yearly risk reports

The World Economic Forum publishes a comprehensive series of reports that examine in detail the broad range of global issues it seeks to address with stakeholders as part of its mission of improving the state of the world. Besides reports on its key events and standalone publications such as the Global Competitiveness Report, the Global Risks Report and the Global Gender Gap Report, the Forum produces landmark titles covering the environment, education, individual industries and technologies.

26.   Life Cycle Analysis (LCA)

LCA is a technique to assess the environmental aspects and potential impacts associated with a product, process, or service, by: compiling an inventory of relevant energy and material inputs and environmental releases. Evaluating the potential environmental impacts associated with identified inputs and releases.

27.   Ecological footprinting

The Ecological Footprint is rooted in the fact that all renewable resources come from the earth. It accounts for the flows of energy and matter to and from any defined economy and converts these into the corresponding land/water area required for nature to support these flows. The Ecological Footprint is defined as "the area of productive land and water ecosystems required producing the resources that the population consumes and assimilate the wastes that the population produces, wherever on Earth the land and water is located." It compares actual throughput of renewable resources relative to what is annually renewed. Non-renewable resources are not assessed, as by definition their use is not sustainable.

28.   Base of the Pyramid strategies

The phrase "Base of the Pyramid" is used for two interrelated concepts: a socio-economic designation for the 4-5 billion individuals that live primarily in developing countries and whose annual per capita incomes fall below $1,500 (in PPP terms); and an emerging field of business strategy that focuses on products, services, and enterprises to serve people throughout the base of the world's income pyramid.

Both concepts are also often referred to as the "Bottom of the Pyramid" or the "BoP".

29.   Human development index

The Human Development Index (HDI) is a composite statistic of life expectancy, education, and income indices used to rank countries into four tiers of human development. It was created by the Pakistani economist Mahbub ul Haq and the Indian economist Amartya Sen in 1990, and was published by the United Nations Development Programme. In the 2010 Human Development Report a further Inequality-adjusted Human Development Index (IHDI) was introduced. While the simple HDI remains useful, it stated that "the IHDI is the actual level of human development (accounting for inequality)" and "the HDI can be viewed as an index of "potential" human development (or the maximum IHDI that could be achieved if there were no inequality)".

30.   6 capitals, as described by IIRC – International Integrated Reporting
       Council

6 capitals are: financial, manufactured, human, intellectual, natural, social. These capitals are the basis of an organization's value creation. In Thriveability

we separate manufactured and infrastructure capital, and social and relationship capital, resulting in 8 capitals.

31.   TEEB

The Economics of Ecosystems and Biodiversity (TEEB) is a global initiative focused on drawing attention to the economic benefits of biodiversity including the growing cost of biodiversity loss and ecosystem degradation. TEEB presents an approach that can help decision-makers recognize, demonstrate and capture the values of ecosystem services & biodiversity.

32.   Reporting 3.0

Reporting 3.0 is a sister movement to Thriveability and shares co-founders. The mission of the Reporting 3.0 Platform is to help catalyze the trigger-function of reporting to spur the emergence of a regenerative and inclusive global economy. To achieve this transformation, Reporting 3.0 curates a collaborative, pre-competitive, neutral space where stakeholders from across the reporting spectrum gather to co-create the design needs and pilot new best practices for future-fit reporting.

Reporting 3.0 is committed to accelerating the emergence of a regenerative & inclusive economy through a series of Blueprint Projects that map out transition pathways in four key areas, co-created by diverse multi-stakeholder Working Groups.

- Reporting – to serve a green and inclusive economy
- Accounting – across the multiple capitals
- Data – integration and contextualization for multicapital accounting
- New Business Models – creation for future-fit value creation and reporting

These four areas are integrated into a fifth blueprint, the Transformation Journey. All blueprints are available at the website below.

33.   https://reporting3.org/

34.   https://en.wikipedia.org/wiki/Clare_W._Graves

35.   https://en.wikipedia.org/wiki/The_Cultural_Creatives

36.   http://www.stockholmresilience.org/research/our-research-focus.html

37.   http://www.footprintnetwork.org/en/index.php/GFN/

38.   http://www.wri.org/news/2012/05/release-international-partners-release-pilot-global-protocol-community-scale-greenhouse

39.   http://www.socialprogressimperative.org/data/spi/findings

40.   http://www.happyplanetindex.org/

41.   http://www.brinq.com/resources/bop

42.   http://www.wbcsd.org/vision2050.aspx

43.   http://www.goodcountry.org/

44.   https://www.globalreporting.org/Pages/default.aspx

45.   http://www.unglobalcompact.org/

46.   http://www.millenniumassessment.org/documents/document.765.asp
x.pdf

47.   http://www.theiirc.org/wp-content/uploads/2013/03/IR-Background-
Paper-Capitals.pdf

48.   http://www.teebweb.org/

49.   http://www.vno-
ncw.nl/SiteCollectionDocuments/Meer%20informatie/deloitte%20csr%2
0onderzoek.pdf

50.   https://www.globalreporting.org/Pages/default.aspx

51.   https://leapfroginvestorsclub.weebly.com/

52.   https://en.wikipedia.org/wiki/Integral_theory_(Ken_Wilber)

53.   http://paulvanschaik.wixsite.com/integralmentors/team

54.   www.rlw.zone

About the Author

Dr Robin Lincoln Wood advises leaders and organisations worldwide on designing and delivering thriveable strategies. Over 4 decades he has worked with hundreds of Global 1000 clients and also created several commercial and socially innovative startups. He focuses on developing leaders and boards capable of delivering thriving futures.

Career History -
https://www.linkedin.com/in/robinlincolnwood/

Personal Website – www.rlw.zone

Other Books by Dr Robin Lincoln Wood

Making Good Happen – Pathways to a Thriving Future - 2017
Synergise! 21st Century Leadership – 2017
A Leaders Guide to ThriveAbility – 2015
The Trouble with Paradise: A Humorous Enquiry Into the Puzzling Human Condition in the 21st Century - 2014
LifeShift 2020 – 2009

The Great Shift: Catalyzing the Second Renaissance - 2009
Managing Complexity:
How Businesses can Adapt and Prosper in the Connected Economy – 2000

Visit the Robin's Amazon page for more details:

www.amazon.com/author/woodrobin

Endnotes

---

[i] The Gini coefficient is a standard measure of income inequality that ranges from 0 (when everybody has identical incomes) to 1 (when all income goes to only one person).

[ii] A New Philosophy of Society: Assemblage Theory and Social Complexity is a 2006 book by Manuel DeLanda. The book is an attempt to loosely define a new ontology for use by social theorists. Delanda employs Gilles Deleuze's theory of assemblages from A Thousand Plateaus (1980) to posit social entities on all scales (from sub-individual to transnational) that are best analysed through their components (themselves assemblages).

[iii] From One Taste by Ken Wilber. https://www.amazon.com/One-Taste-Reflections-Integral-Spirituality/dp/1570625476

[iv] Something we chronicled in "A Leader's Guide to ThriveAbility" in 2015. http://bit.ly/LeadersGuidetoThriveAbility-Kindle

[v] https://www2.deloitte.com/au/en/pages/consumer-business/articles/the-growth-of-aqua-culture-fishy-business.html

[vi] https://www.pwc.com/us/en/technology/publications/assets/pwc-consumer-intelligence-series-the-sharing-economy.pdf